MARIA ZEF

Translated and with an introduction

by Blossom Steinberg Kirschenbaum

Paola Drigo:

Maria Zef

University of Nebraska Press: Lincoln & London

Published in Italian
as *Maria Zef,*
copyright © Garzanti
Editore s.p.a.,
1939, 1982

The paper in
this book meets the
minimum
requirements of
American
National Standard
for Information
Sciences – Perma-
nence of Paper
for Printed Library
Materials,
ANSI Z39.48-1984.

Library of Congress
Cataloging
in Publication Data
Drigo, Paola,
1876-1938.
Maria Zef.
(European women
writers series)
Translated from
the Italian.
Translation of:
Maria Zef.
I. Title.   II. Series
PQ4811.R5M3I3   1989
853'.912   88-37837
ISBN 0-8032-1676-9
(alk. paper)
ISBN 0-8032-6577-8
(pbk: alk. paper)

*P*aola Drigo (1876–1938) was born in the medieval town of Castelfranco in the Veneto. Daughter of *garibaldino* Valerio Bianchetti of Asolo, wife of an engineer from Mussolente (Bassano del Grappa), she was herself from comfortable circumstances. Yet she wrote of humble characters, the *diseredati,* revealing the drama of their lives and their profound humanity. Poverty, hunger, privation, and mistreatment are conditions that did not afflict her personally, but emotionally she shared them. Her fiction is religious in spirit. She conveys the sanctity of life, and searingly and compassionately she shows how that sanctity can be violated. The spirit that animates her work is a rejection of complacency while others suffer.

Drigo's modest oeuvre consists of three collections of stories: *La Fortuna,* 1913; *Codino,* 1918; and *La Signorina Anna,* 1932; a volume of poetry, *Col mio infinito,* 1921; a brief memoir *Fine d'anno,* 1936; and the one novel that is her masterpiece. *Maria Zef,* published in 1936, two years before her death, was both a critical and a popular success. A final story, 'Window on the River,' about Padua, where Drigo had spent the previous winter, was written in the hospital the summer before she died. A single bibliographic source lists a work of fiction called *La signorina di Friours,* 1929.

Perhaps *Maria Zef* faded from attention because the author died a mere two years after its publication. Then came the war and a flood of postwar writing. Contemporaries rediscovered the book and reissued it in 1982. (There may have been a reprinting in 1953.) *Maria Zef* was twice translated into film: a 1954 version directed by Luigi De Marchi, released under both the original title and as *Condannata senza colpa*, and a 1981 film made for RAI-TV3, produced by the Friuli regional government and directed by Vittorio Cottafava.

In the Veneto that Drigo describes, an agricultural economy dominated until well into the twentieth century, resisting industrialization. The presence of a thread factory is noted in *Maria Zef* as having absorbed almost all the local work force, but the landscape is generally rural and preindustrial. Along the banks of the Livenza and the Piave rivers, Mariutine sees homesteads, haystacks, and stables. Clusters of houses have some distance between them, and it is communal activities like harvesting, carnival, and fairs that bring people together. Farming is not yet mechanized and goods are transported by horse and wagon. Drigo wrote of a vitiated aristocracy, prospering dairy farmers, healthy, good-hearted enterprising countryfolk constrained by circumstances and forced to make difficult decisions, and emigrant laborers who sometimes returned.

The wind and the mountain are two features that figure importantly in her lucid narrative style, as she renders the drama of daily life with a dry compassionate humor and a strict lyricism. She presents survival through life-threatening crises in harsh landscapes not ruled by human will, looking on, as critic Manara Valgimigli wrote, with an unwavering implacable eye. Winter was her favorite season: bare branches, clear outlines, a world reduced to essentials, austere. Her landscape is one of inhuman solitude and silence. In the rigors of winter, mountains have no pity. Mariutine's plea for refuge in her time of trouble (*'Dove, dove, dove, trovare asilo e pietà,'* reads the Italian)

viii

gets no response from them. As against an indifferent nature, Drigo presents life as risen from the mud. At epiphanic moments, the interpenetrating levels of animal, human, and divine perfectly merge. In her dispassion, she seems bent simply on stirring the responsive heart to a sense of the sacred.

Friuli, the setting of this novel, is in extreme northeastern Italy, a twofold terrain of alpine mountains (Carnia) and watered plain, corresponding now to the province of Udine. Ethnically, it is a confluence of Mediterranean, Danubian, and Slavic peoples. Feudalism favored Germanic penetration: in 1382 the Catholic church supported a French ruler; later Udine asked aid from Venice, provoking intervention of the King of Hungary, long hostile to Venetian expansion. Still later the region passed to Hapsburg rule—and again to Austria under Maria Teresa. After World War II tensions between Italy and Yugoslavia caused administrative boundaries to be redrawn, and in 1954 the zone administered by the Allies formally passed to Italy. This history, much abbreviated here of course, influences every aspect of local culture— artifacts, speech, and surviving traditions.

People of Friuli are said to endure harsh climates, adapt readily to other places, work hard, keep their word, and tolerate isolation. As immigrants, the men fell trees in the Canadian forests, mine for iron in polar regions, take up residence in villages hundreds of kilometers from the nearest town. Other workers ask to be sent back, or require long weekends, or flee to the restaurants of Montreal or Toronto—but not immigrants from Carnia! Their strength is also their fault: to labor always for others, as they had labored always in their own harsh ungrateful native terrain. In the same way centuries earlier masons of Carnia had in Hungary built fortifications for protecting Europe from the Turks—had built half of Vienna and almost all of Trieste under Maria Teresa, had worked in St.

Petersburg and Sevastopol for the czar—and so on also in South America and in Africa. Their outstanding qualities, both strength and limitation, might be disdained in cultural centers like Venice and Trieste. Stolid and industrious, the mountain people of Carnia and the peasants from the plains of the Tagliamento River made their contributions as builders, caretakers, and domestics—'a people who resolve many problems but do not create any.'

D. B. Gregor's 1965 essay 'Friulan: the Language of Friuli,' published in England, begins with the statement: 'Italians are bilingual, and their second language is Italian.' Dialect, the regional mother tongue, the language of early basic feelings and thoughts, best expresses those deepest, most resonant emotions, as well as the isolation in which they developed, and attachment to place. Gregor names villages that persist in their own dialectical gradations and cites six regularly observed changes within only ten miles, commenting, 'If a language must have a title to existence it has it in being the reflection of a community's soul.' Gregor calls Friulan 'a dialect of Italy without being an Italian dialect' and analyzes its formation and grammar, established about one thousand years ago. A literature evolved that includes works by Count Ernesto di Colloredo (1622–92, the 'Friulan Dante'), poet Pietro Zorutti (1792–1867), Caterina Percoto (1812–87, 'la contessa contadina'), F. Cornelli (1826–92), and poet-scholar Bindo Chiurlo (1886–1943, who 'made accessible many of the little known works of the past, co-founded the Società Filologica Friulana, and edited its publication *Ce fas-tu*'). To his essay Gregor appends an anthology of short selections in prose and verse.

Though Gregor does not refer to Pier Paolo Pasolini, Olga Ragusa and other critics writing at about the same time refer to Pasolini's stay during World War II in Casarsa, his mother's village in Friuli. His earliest poems were in dialect, 'inspired,' as Ragusa notes, 'by his love for the simple, instinctive peasant life of a rural region that progress had bypassed, the same region that a century earlier served as setting for Nievo's wonderful *contes champêtres*.' Pasolini also published an anthology of Italian dialect poetry. Especially, I suppose, because I remain attached to my own thousand-year-old ancestral language, which survives the near eradication of Europeans who spoke it and continues to be taught at universities like Columbia and Oxford, I feel an innate resistance to the loss of any people's speech, and so am pleased to call attention to Friulan.

Particularly, as in this book, where thousands of miles and years of time will separate sweethearts, the shared language and songs constitute a bond and a promise. The *villotta* is often about love even though other themes also emerge. This *canto lirico monostrofico* (in verses of four octosyllabic lines with alternately weak and rhyming strong endings—thousands of them have been collected) originated in Friulan. I have translated with meter and rhyme the *villotte* that Mariutine sings as she wanders and that Pieri too will sing in his wanderings, though I could not find an American equivalent for the dialect itself. The songs express, in my opinion, not only Mariutine's attachment to her spiritual home ground and her primary emotional ties, but the very connections that make folk all over the world resist linguistic assimilation. I think the songs also express Paola Drigo's love for the austere, difficult, beautiful region.

In translating I kept some words and phrases of dialect: the vendor's cry *càndole e candolini;* the word for the wrapped-cloth slippers *scarputis;* the debated term *usgnòt;* foods like the thick soup *jote* and the balls of ground pork liver *martondella* and the simple cheese *çuc;* also I kept *mâri, frute,* and the parting 'so long,' *mandi.* These words, distinguished by italic type in the Italian text, are left intact in the English translation to confirm the particularity of geographic and cultural setting.

I have kept two idiosyncrasies of Drigo's style that seem symbolic. One is her use of the series of three terms (nouns or adjectives) not separated by commas: 'two women a handcart and a dog'; 'washed combed and with her limbs composed'; 'swollen turbid and plundering'; and so forth. These triplets, as I think of them, seem to reinforce the triple levels of subhuman, human, and superhuman in her worldview. I have therefore kept the triplets without commas. Drigo also has a way of doubling a term: 'tightly tightly,' 'very very,' 'a fine little calf, a fine little calf.' I keep this mannerism because it seems deliberately employed to intensify and insist on the life of the moment.

Friuli has a history of women writers dating back to Irene da Spilimbergo, petrarchist, and in the 1700s Giulia Arcoloniani and Teresa Zai, mystics. Caterina Percoto wrote in both Italian and dialect very much as a woman. Maria Barbina and Geda Jacolutti list outstanding turn-of-the-century and early twentieth-century women writers, including nationally noted Maria Luisa Astaldi, who also left a modern art collection to the city of Udine. A new literary flow followed World War II—and then, in the wave of self-consideration of women, many other voices arose. Say Barbina and Jacolutti, 'These writers were connected neither to the Academiuta (founded by Pasolini) nor the Friulan neorealism, even where the vocabulary was similar and there were resemblances to Pasolini. Women had trouble infiltrating the all-male intellectual circles, of course, and couldn't always be so free with their time; moreover, they conceived of art as an element of liberation and of recognition of their own human values—not as pedagogic, political, moralistic, or rhetorical, but an active gratification linking one to landscape, other people, and a better life—modifying the landscape.' As women from this region and throughout Italy continue to publish, Drigo will probably loom as a major predecessor.

Gualtiero Amici ranks Drigo on the same artistic plane, for *Maria Zef,* with Matilde Serao and Nobelist Grazia Deledda. For contemporary readers in a secular and distractingly materialistic society, the spiritually evocative and resonant realism of this novel may astonishingly illuminate, reassure, and comfort.

*

This translation is dedicated to my daughters Jennet Diana and Helena April and my son Abram Eugene; to my niece and nephew Nancy and Daniel Steinberg; to Rachel Hass and Kathryn Schwertman.

ACKNOWLEDGMENTS

I should like to thank Simonetta and Lodovico Branca, who discussed this book with me when I had only just begun translating it, and Giacomo Striuli, who read portions of a late version of the manuscript. Those conversations have been great pleasures in my life.

Francesco Zerlenga at the Istituto Italiano di Cultura in New York kindly allowed me to use the library and made many supportive comments. Timothy Troy, reference librarian at the New York Public Library on Fifth Avenue, responded to my urgent pleas by sending photocopied pages of a Friulan-Italian dictionary and helped me also when I came in person to pursue researches; I am especially happy to thank him, because his mother and I were colleagues in teaching and his father as book editor of the *Providence Journal-Bulletin* published my reviews. Piergiuseppe Bozzetti, cultural attaché at the Italian Embassy in Washington, reassured me that I had correctly translated the *villotte* before I cast them into meter and rhyme in English.

Franco Fido and Anthony Oldcorn of Brown University encouraged me with benevolence and great good humor, and Olga Ragusa of Columbia University offered patiently the benefits of her far deeper knowledge than mine and her close empathetic reading of Paola Drigo's masterpiece; she also helped me contain the Introduction, which at one time was thrice as long.

As for the other colleagues and friends and members of my family who stood by and sometimes cheered: they know who they are! Of course I take full responsibility for any residual flaws.

Blossom Steinberg Kirschenbaum

*T*here were two women a handcart and a dog. They went along the embankment of the river, after sunset, toward the scattered houses of a large hamlet on the opposite bank from which some lights could just barely be seen glimmering.

The two-wheeled cart, loaded with ladles, bowls, *càndole* and *candolini,* candlesticks and sconces, and other items made of wood, was drawn along by one of the women, who, bound to the shafts by means of a belt that passed under her armpits, strained forward bravely, avoiding the ruts and the mud along the way.

Actually, though tall and well built with a mountain woman's broad shoulders, she was really more girl than woman, scarcely thirteen or fourteen years old, with a round and naive little face, and two expressively childlike blue eyes.

Even while steadfastly continuing to perform her role of cart horse, she turned from time to time with obvious anxiety to look at her mother, who, walking alongside the cart and keeping a hand on the edge of it as though to push it forward, was in fact wearily leaning against it, laboriously dragging along her broad feet encased in the cloth slippers called *scarputis,* typical of Friuli.

On closer inspection, it could be seen that a third person also belonged to this party, a little girl of five or six, sunk deep in sleep among the ladles and candlesticks, and

3

wrapped up in a tattered old shawl from which stuck out only a lock of red hair and the outline of a chubby cheek. A dog, a little poodle the color of mud trotting along with them, completed the small convoy.

*

They had been walking since dawn and had walked also the day before and the day before that and even the day previous to that one, for the past two weeks, crossing a great expanse of the region that descends from Friuli to the sea.

They broke their journey in settlements, at fairs, and in the courtyards of farmhouses, to sell their merchandise. They ate, it can be said, while walking along, and they slept wherever they happened to arrive: in the porches of homesteads, in haystacks, in stables.

Nearing a cluster of houses, the older girl announced herself by a little chant: '*Càndole, candolini,* kitchenware, tableware, ladies!'

Then the peasant women of the valley, florid and stout, would come out from their houses with infants and youngsters clinging to their skirts. Curious, they gathered around the cart. Finally they bought, for petty sums, after long discussions, one woman this item and another that.

*

The mother and her young daughters were already well known throughout the whole countryside along the banks of the Livenza and the Piave, since, coming down every year from the Carnia region at the beginning of autumn, they always passed by more or less the same places. They did not return to the mountains until after they had emptied the cart and scraped together a little hoard of money for the winter.

When they were passing by, the good countrypeople called out to them by name and greeted them cheerily: 'Catine! Mariùte! Rosùte!'

The children ran over to them laughing and shouting: 'Uh, Mariùte! Uh, Rosùte! Uh, Catine!'

To tell the truth, Catine, the mother, would not have inspired either sympathy or cheer, since she was a woman of glum appearance, silent, always shivering with cold, and with a dark kerchief tied under her chin like an old woman.

She may not have been as old as she looked, but she was so worn out and run down as to seem decrepit. She coughed continually, and she dragged her feet as she walked, seeming to make hard work even out of answering whoever greeted her. She broke out of her torpor only to argue obstinately about the price of her merchandise. Then, two ruddy spots at her temples kindled her deathly pallor, her voice quavered, and her mouth trembled around toothless gums. Mariutine, the elder daughter, watched her, timidly anxious. The peasant women murmured: 'What a grouch!'

With her way of doing things, Catine would doubtless have disgusted and alienated her clientele, enough to make them keep their distance, if she had not had Mariutine beside her. But at difficult moments Mariutine knew how to interrupt with a conciliating or playful word that neutralized, so to speak, the resistance aroused by the mother. Then too she had an art, that girl, for inveigling even those who didn't want to do so to buy something!

She picked up the items ever so daintily, handling them by her fingertips as though they were made of gold. She turned them over and turned them around to display them from every angle, showing off their good qualities and concealing their defects. She looked potential buyers full in the face, with those blue eyes of hers that, even while laughing, implored.

'Oh, it's hard to believe those young girls are the children of that infernal hag,' said the women. 'Mariutine's a sweetheart, a golden girl, yet she even does duty as a cart horse. Rosùte, why she's made of butter!'

In fact, the youngsters were lovely, well built, and of

rosy complexion. Everybody liked the girls: Mariutine clever, nimble, and merry, dauntless against cold, hunger, sleepiness, and fatigue; Rosùte, so funny, with her shock of red hair sticking straight up, bundled into a man's old jacket, chubby and placid as if she fed on dainty baked thrushes and warblers instead of on stale bread. People did not even realize that she was lame, though she was not actually that either: she had hurt her foot while going barefoot, and when she got down from the cart she favored the injury, keeping her little paw of a foot lifted up in the air, as do storks.

'Càndole, candolini, kitchenware, tableware, ladies!'

Occasionally, in good years, when they happened by some wealthy farmhouse at the time of the grape harvest, when the table was set not only for the master and his family, but also for the field hands, and an immense cauldron of soup was steaming on the fire, the good-hearted farmwife would set extra places, adding a bowl and a hunk of bread for them too, accommodating them at the table along with the grape harvesters.

For Mariutine, these were great feast days. The laden table was set under the portico, bearing a homespun cloth and flower-patterned bowls, and along the table there were not chairs, but long, narrow wooden benches. At the rear under the portico the cellar spread wide open, long and mysterious as a cave, with its black rafters, its immense vats, and men in shirtsleeves coming out of it. Hanging from a hook was an oil lamp whose flame wavered with the drafts of air. It lit up the cellar with a reddish light, leaving large areas in shadow.

When the sky began to turn pale, the disheveled women harvesters would hurry back, bringing the last baskets of grapes. Like huge devils the grape crushers would leap out from their vats and run to the fountain to wash off the red grape must from their hairy legs. The farmwife, conscious of her importance, would ladle out soup into the bowls. Then the cat emerged watchful from under the plough, and the dog crouched, wagging his tail, next to the seat of the master of the house. After a moment of disorderly scrambling, shoving, and laughter, there was suddenly a great silence. Everyone bent over a plate and ate greedily, looking neither right nor left. But after having eaten, there was always someone who said: 'Sing something for us, Mariutine!'

And Mariutine, blushing a bit, but without having to be coaxed, would nimbly step over the bench and run out into the middle of the courtyard:

> *Well, good evening everybody!*
> *Do please give me your consent*
> *Just to sing a dance tune for you*
> *Without causing discontent.*

> *If you know the chorus to it*
> *I will sing along with you*
> *But if no one knows the words then*
> *Just lalìn-lalà will do.*

'Lalìn-lalà! Lalìn-lalà!' repeated the harvesters in chorus, stamping their feet and clapping their hands.

And she:

> *Singing never makes one weary*
> *Not unless someone is ill,*
> *As for one who's really heartsick,*
> *What'll cheer him? Singing will!*

> *Singing never makes one weary,*
> *Except the grouch who's full of sighs,*
> *So we sing to bring good cheer to*
> *Those whom passions agonize.*

The young girl cut a gawky figure. She was alone in the middle of the big courtyard, in her wide skirt, shoulders enveloped by a worn shawl whose ends crossed on her

7

breast. Her contours were ill defined, but her small head, wrapped around by tight braids of glinting blond, stood out delicate and luminous under the pale sky where the first stars were beginning to appear.

'Sing us another one, Mariutine, another one: and this time *longer!*' Her listeners would clap their hands.

And she was ready, laughing with her clever eyes, and, lifting up the corners of her apron with a fingertip, she would make a little curtsey:

We will sing no more this evening,
Of songs I know you've heard full store.
Do come back tomorrow evening,
By then I will've learned some more.

Now it's time to say good evening
Now it's time to say good night
Do come back another evening,
We'll sing better than tonight.

'*Chantarin plui ben di usgnòt,*' she concluded the folk song, in her native Friulan.

At these sallies, the little children and the boys, lively scamps no older than fifteen or so, would come running around Mariutine making a hellish row.

'*Usgnòt! Usgnòt!* What's the meaning of *usgnòt?*'

From the grape harvesters, squatting on their heels around the courtyard, a voice would answer back: 'It's a singing bird! It's a nightingale!'

'*Usgnòt*' doesn't really mean 'usignole,' which in Friulan dialect is called simply 'nightingale,' but Mariùte, deafened from the merry cries, surrounded and pursued across the courtyard, had no time to give explanations.

Oh, it would have pleased her enormously to stay on singing longer, to laugh among the swarm of children her own age, but she met her mother's sad eyes, and saw her tired face, old, white lipped. Catine said nothing at all, but Mariùte lost all courage to resume her song.

The moon was already rising large and round in the sky, and beneath its glimmer the fields and hedges glistened as though soaking wet. There hovered over the countryside that sort of stupefaction, that sort of dreaminess, that precedes nighttime. The air became cold. The mother needed to stretch out at last, even if only on two armfuls of straw next to the animals in the stable, so as to have the strength to walk again the next day. She would not have wanted to go to sleep without Mariutine and Rosùte, for, brusque and indifferent with people in general, she had a fierce passion for her own flesh and blood, and a jealous vigilance. She would not move even a step away from them. It seemed to give her no pleasure at all that Mariutine should sing; but how to prevent her from doing it?

Mariutine, if she could have, would have sung from dawn to dusk, like a young bird. She knew a great many folk songs, *villotte,* which she had learned on her own, making up all sorts of variations, and provocative flourishes and question-and-answer returns, as was customary in the valleys where she came from. For her it was the greatest happiness to be asked to sing a *villotta.* It seemed to her that had she been able to sing while pulling the cart, she would no longer have felt weary or tired. Maybe she would not even have felt that awful pain caused by the leather strap binding her around under the armpits. What pain it inflicted, that horrible rubbing leather strap. . . . Between her arms and small breasts, it had gouged a black-and-blue welt, which sometimes chafed so hard that it bled. But no one knew that: no, there was no need to tell anyone. Her mother especially must not know. . . . Her mother would have wanted to pull the cart herself in that case, as before, in an earlier time when Mariutine was too small to have the strength for it, poor, poor mother!

But it was really not possible to sing while pulling. The roads were bad: holes, gravel, mud; the cart weighed a lot; to draw it along required pushing the head forward, hunching the shoulders. No, impossible! . . . Of necessity Mariutine had to be content with singing when they asked her to as payment for a bit of bread and whatever went with the bread, or during their stops along the way, while Catine was washing their few tattered garments in the water running alongside the road.

At such times her baby sister and the poodle were Mariutine's only audience, but they were enough for her.

Oh lofty windows barred and shuttered
If you could speak and witness bear!
But what I said to my little darling
No one else will ever hear.

Always too soon, it seemed, her mother said: 'Let's go, Mariùte.'

And again they took to the road.

✳

Besides that, despite weariness, their wandering pleased Mariutine very much. She loved this type of adventurous enterprise, which every year pried her from their cabin to push along the world's broad open highways.

That lovely open spreading countryside, how rich and cheerful it was in contrast with the bare dryness of the mountains where she was born—and in comparison too with the steep vales where her isolated cabin nestled! . . . Of course, the treks were arduous. She had to toil terribly hard to eke out a living and scrape together a little money, but every year ended in some success, and each day was different from the other. She went, she went, along the wide river, between the broad fields, among vineyards and apple orchards, meadows and streams, and she looked around and greeted everything with inquisitive and smiling eyes, and every house had a courtyard for her performances as a singer, and in the courtyard, evenings, sometimes she danced by moonlight.

In their travels they met almost every year a certain blindman. He went around from one region to another like them, with his accordion strapped across his shoulders, guided only by his dog. The two made a long tour, and at harvesttime they stopped off in just about all the farmsteads to get the young people dancing. With his head thrown back and an ecstatic expression in his blank eyes, the blindman played. The dog, with a little plate in his mouth, upright on his hind legs, went around to collect the offerings.

Actually, no one invited Mariutine to dance. She was still too much a child and perhaps too poor and ill clad to flatter the vanity of the village farm boys, but she was not in the least bothered by this. She had a good time all the same watching the others dance; she was a joyous and vigorous young creature, incapable of envy or meanness.

That year, though, had been a quite sad year. Drought had burned up the harvests, and drought was followed by a period of torrential rains that transformed the countryside into a vast swamp.

By day, the houses and trees emerged grey and ghostly from the mud. Then, toward evening, the mist swathed them around, first light and wavering like a veil, then ever more heavy and drooping, equalizing everything in its opaque infinite melancholy.

Turbid and menacing, the river flowed between desolate banks. The road after sunset was hazardous for the traveler, since the river and the plain could no longer be told apart. They were mixed together and confounded in the treacherous immensity of the fog.

People of the countryside had no money to spend, that year, not even for bread. They hadn't stored grapes and wine; just imagine whether they were in the mood to buy 'càndole and candolini.' Wooden ladles and bowls interested them even less, for, to buy bowls, said the women, one must have something to put into them.

Catine and the girls no longer dared ask for shelter at the farmsteads, where even the dogs reacted rancorously and with rude bursts of barking. They would wait outside, rather, under whatever roof or abandoned lean-to was available, until a pause between one cloudburst and the next, and then continue on their way. Their itinerary was almost done, and the cart was still full of goods.

'This year the Friulans might have saved themselves the trip,' grumbled the farm women crossly, watching them pass by and preferring to avoid any kind of greeting to them.

Uselessly Mariutine flung out her cry: 'Càndole, candolini, kitchenware, tableware, ladies!'

No voice replied. The houses appeared deserted. Most of the men had gone abroad in search of work. The countryside seemed a cemetery. There was only misery all around, misery and water. It was useless to persist in carrying all that merchandise around just for the sake of taking it for a ride, stuff that nobody wanted to buy.

✳

One day, beyond the built-up area, Catine and Mariùte, as if by tacit agreement, pushed the cart to one side of the road and sat down on a pile of gravel. Catine drew from her bosom a little leather pouch that she carried fastened around her neck by a string between shift and skin, and she poured its contents into her daughter's lap.

'Count,' she told her.

And Mariutine counted. There were thick copper coins, almost black, mixed in among some nickel ones and a few pieces of silver.

'Twenty-seven and forty. I must have made a mistake, mâri!' exclaimed the child. And with keen attention, the copper separated from the nickel, the nickel from the silver, in three tiny little piles, she counted again. The mother followed her daughter's movements with feverish eyes, stretching forward her scrawny neck.

'Twenty-seven and forty . . . ' repeated Mariutine in a low and quivering voice.

She stared at her mother, and would not meet her gaze. Neither one nor the other uttered a word. Catine slowly replaced the coins in the pouch and hid it again in her bosom. Then, seeing that Rosùte had got to splashing around in a puddle, she gave her a violent tug and lifted her back up onto the cart. 'Forward,' she commanded harshly.

They went on another kilometer or two. They reached the Piave, and passed it, without encountering either houses or human beings. Night fell. They came into a dairy shed, a sort of abandoned storehouse. Besides a pile of straw, two old cases broken in pieces, and some rusted hoops, there were fresh horse turds scattered on the ground and the remains of a campfire that indicated the recent stopover of some horse-and-wagon driver.

Rosùte with great joy picked up an empty match tin decorated with a colored picture. Mariutine, after having piled up the straw litter at a good distance, bunched together some sticks, painstakingly kindled a fire, and called to her mother to come warm herself.

But Catine had already huddled in a corner. She had wished neither to eat nor to warm herself. Instead, she had drawn her shawl up over her eyes and appeared to be asleep. Knowing her mother's silences, the girl had not dared to insist. She only glanced over from time to time, uneasy.

From the damp litter, from the soaked planks that made up the shed, and from their own very garments, at the blazing up of the fire there arose a light vapor, like a breath, that remained suspended in midair. Squatting near the flame, Mariutine and Rosùte bit greedily into their bread. They gave a little piece of it to the poodle, who stared at them with human eyes. Then Rosùte drew from her pocket a sour apple, which was just a bite for one, and, laughing, they gobbled it up together in mere moments.

Much later, Rosùte called in a subdued tone: 'Mariutine . . . '

Mariutine was awake, but she pretended not to hear.

'Mariutine . . . '

'What's the matter?'

'I'm scared of the mice.'

'There aren't any. Sleep,' ordered Mariutine firmly. But, reaching out to grope for her sister's hand, she stroked it, pressed it, holding it authoritatively in her own.

'Lie closer to me: this way . . . ' begged Rosùte, and, heaving a sigh of relief, she made no delay in falling asleep.

But, deep down, Mariutine too, was afraid. The day before, she herself had also seen one of those mice that Rosùte was scared of, a mouse almost as fat as a cat, a filthy thing, come out from a sewer.

From her straw pallet, in the darting light of the dying campfire, she seemed to make out the uncertain shape of one of them, hear it coming warily nearer and nearer along the walls, and tightly tightly she gathered up her clothes around her body and did not dare close her eyes. She fought against sleep and against tiredness, stiffened with loathing, motionless, straining her ears for noises.

No, nothing. Only the rain that poured down with uninterrupted violence on the shed's zinc roof. Inundated, all the other voices of the countryside were hushed.

'But what would mice ever want to be doing here,' thought Mariutine reassuring herself, 'here where there is absolutely nothing to eat? If anything, those mice prefer to roam around outdoors, where they can find something. . . . And besides, there's Petòti to keep guard.'

Petòti was the dog, but he was such a timid and affectionate animal and so remote from violent acts, that, at the appearance of a mouse, he would have gone to meet it wagging his tail rather than engaging in battle, and the mouse would have made a single dainty morsel of him. No, it was not possible to count on Petòti.

During that night, between vigil and sleep—or maybe in a dream?—at one point it seemed to Mariutine that she heard something like a suppressed sigh, a moan. She lifted herself alert on her pallet to listen, but she could hear nothing more.

The rain had ceased. From the nearby and faraway ponds began the immense concerto of the frogs. They called to each other, they replied to each other; one voice rose up, in a solo, and a chorus of innumerable voices followed. And in the unexpected interval of silence, the countryside appeared immense, boundless; suspended in the deepest peace.

✳

Next day at dawn, Mariutine was up and about. She had had a bad night and felt tired, as though all her bones were broken. Yet when she looked out from the storehouse door an unforeseen spectacle astounded her, making her heart beat high with joy.

It was the sun—a meek, faraway sun—that tried to penetrate the thick and dense feather bed of clouds. The meadows were steaming; a warm slight breeze stirred the branches of the trees. Some small bird hopped up on the hedge shaking its feathers; in the middle of the swollen Piave, the *grave,* or ripples, glistened like immense rafts streaked with silver. It was returning! Brightness was returning!

She saw a bucket half full of rainwater. She washed. She rebraided her hair neatly. She tidied up the cart; she checked the leather belt and noticed that it was dry, stiff on account of the heavy rain that had soaked into it. She looked for and found, under the candlesticks, the little container of grease, and she oiled the belt with meticulous care while singing in an undertone:

Oh lofty windows barred and shuttered
If you could speak and witness bear!
But what I said to my little darling
No one else will ever hear.

In a few moments her mother and Rosùte too were ready.

Strapped in place between the shafts of the cart, trotting boldly on ahead, Mariutine peered up at the sky, turned intermittently to look to her sister, and winked at her with those blue eyes, barely restraining herself from neighing like a little horse. She would have liked at least to cry out, 'There's the sun! There's the sun!' But she did not dare, for fear of her mother.

And now suddenly, when they'd hardly more than gotten started, Catine collapsed in the middle of the road, and she began to sob, brokenly and frantically.

During the past days, she had been worse off than ever before. Pain at the tip of the shoulder blade that had been tormenting her for a long time had become acute, unbearable, like a dagger stabbing away at her back. Long shudders shook her from head to foot, and she was so terribly thirsty, so terribly tired . . .

At the first outburst of that lament, Mariutine, who had already moved on some distance ahead, abruptly halted, blanched, impulsively unhitched the belt from around her shoulders, ran to her mother, and knelt down beside her on the ground.

'*Mâri!* . . . *Mâri!* . . . *Mâri!* . . .' she repeated entreatingly, embracing her with both arms, stroking her hair, her face, her hands. 'There's sunshine now, *mâri!* . . . Why should you cry? Why are you crying, *mâri?* . . .'

Rosùte, sitting up amid the candlesticks with a finger in her mouth, watched in perplexity this one and the other, in silence. Then she too began to whimper quietly without quite knowing why.

Of course, not even at that moment did Mariutine

recognize the full seriousness and implications of her mother's illness. For a long time now just watching her had brought pain to her heart. It had interrupted her in the middle of her singing, but she had believed that what wore her mother down so was above all the thought of the return home, the return without money.

'You'll see, you'll see, Mother. We'll sell even what's left, we'll sell everything, before we get home . . . ' she whispered into her mother's ear, kissing her and caressing her. 'There's the Sacile fair coming, you remember, Mother? . . . That big fair, with so many booths, with so many people . . . You know how good I am at selling. We'll manage this time too. We'll earn what we need to earn, we'll make out. Like every year: you'll see, Mother. Cheer up, stop crying. You'll see, Mother, you'll see!'

All at once, while she was speaking, and while she was lightly touching her smooth face to her mother's and touching her face to her mother's cold hands, and to that body convulsed by an unrelenting tremor, dread overcame her, took her breath away; dread, terror, horror of something that she didn't yet completely fathom, but that was present. 'Something' was with them, 'something' was between them; and against it, nothing could avail.

'Mâri, mâri!' she called then, grasping her mother by the shoulders, holding her at arm's length the better to look her in the face. *'Mâri!'* she called, almost at the top of her voice. 'Mamma, answer me, tell me what's wrong! . . . Are you thirsty? . . . Do you want me to give you a sip of water? Do you want me to cover you with my shawl? Do you want to lie down on the cart? . . . Yes, Mamma, yes. Don't cry any more; hold on; now I'll carry you. I'll carry you. Your hands are so cold. You won't have to walk any further. You're tired. You need to rest. You'll rest. Hold on, Mamma. But tell me, tell me what you want me to do, Mamma dear!'

All around them there was not a living soul. There was

only the grey sky, the grey countryside, over which passed a lone bird in its low and heavy flight.

And Catine cried no more, nor did she reply. Perhaps she did not hear. She cast the glance of her widened transfixed eyes on her young ones filled with infinite despair.

A wagon came passing by. The drayman was on foot walking alongside his horse, whistling, with a pack on his back. He was a good fellow; he stopped his wagon abruptly to see what might be the matter with those two young girls all sopping wet, who were making such a to-do around the woman stretched out on the ground. The bigger one was trying unsuccessfully to prop up and lift the woman, to help her get up. The little one was crying away while tears kept gushing down endlessly. Even the dog yowled and writhed in despair.

'Has she gotten hurt, that woman? . . . No? Only not feeling well? Sick? . . . Is she out of breath? . . . Hey, okay, you don't have to carry on like this.'

He was willing to set her on his wagon, atop the sacks of cement, and take her to the nearby town. There was a doctor there, the pharmacy, the hospital. And the cart, with all its stuff? . . . Oh, his horse, loaded down as it was, couldn't possibly take off at a run. Mariutine, without hurrying overmuch, could manage quite well to take her place behind the horse, with her little cart, following her mother.

The good man had lifted Catine like a heap of rags—uh, light as a feather!—and had put her down on his wagon; he stretched a piece of oilcloth over her when that accursed rain started up again. Mariutine put her little woolen shawl beneath her mother's head. As for the baby, the drayman had cheerily picked her up and held her on one arm while she clung to his neck, and with his free hand he had given one sharp crack of the whip, and off they went!

Catine was sent to the hospital that very evening. In truth, this was an out-and-out irregularity, an exception to the rule, the hospital being reserved for the poor of the township, not for outsiders or transients. But the seriousness of the poor woman's condition, obvious at once to the doctor, and the remoteness from her own home region had been factors recommending, after some hesitation on his part, that he make concessions with regard to applying the letter of the law. They took her in. By this point, however, there was no more to be done.

Bilateral pleurisy, aggravated by conditions of general exhaustion.'

How that unfortunate woman had been able just a short time before to stand up, speak, and walk, in that state of weakness and malnutrition, and with those deep extensive lesions of the lungs, was really beyond comprehension.

And, by the irony of fate, now that she finally did have a bed, a shelter, a hot water bottle on her icy knees, she took a sharp turn for the worse. She had just barely been in time to receive the holy sacraments. At dawn she breathed her last.

*

From papers found in her pocket, they learned her name, surname, and where she came from. A telegram was sent to the authorities of her township for emergency instructions with regard to the burial and sending home the orphans. While awaiting news and instructions, the local people gossiped freely about the 'pitiful case.'

Rather than a village or small town, this was an area of rural homesteads spread over the plains, enjoying a certain prosperity and not too much troubled by either drought or flood. A thread factory had absorbed almost all the work force thereabouts. It was also a lucky region, because nothing ever happened there: no scandals, no bankruptcies, no pestilences, no suicides. It was a region where, moreover, for a whole decade no one had died: indeed, on account of this fact, it had been mentioned in the newspaper *Corriere della Sera*.

In such a dearth of notable events, the touching story of Catine and the two little orphan girls excited a great fuss. And it touched especially the imagination and the compassionate hearts of the women. They wanted to go to see the dead Catine, washed combed and with her limbs composed as she had never looked while alive. They wanted to get to know the little orphan girls, and after many kisses and caresses they made a gift to them of two frocks of black woolen cloth, a fine pair of new shoes, and two inexplicable bonnets.

The men meanwhile, in the café or in the pharmacy, held heated discussions, and, in spite of the proprieties, very nearly came to blows.

'Haven't they proceeded yet to do an autopsy? This is a case of sudden death.'

'Almost sudden.'

'Come on now, sudden. A pleurisy diagnosed with the greatest and utmost precision. She had been carrying it around for six months.'

'And even something more than that, it seems . . . ' insinuated the other one who seemed to have inside information, lowering his voice. 'I'm not sure if I get my meaning across. . . . These women tramping around, whose men go abroad to find work. . . . This one too . . . ' and he leaned close to his neighbor's ear to complete the sentence.

'In any case, instructions have to come from her own people back home. We have to be careful, by God, in such delicate matters.'

But because the instructions were slow in coming or were jumbled and contradictory—it seemed that the dead woman had no relatives or that none cared about her fate—and especially after the rains, when a warm southern wind had begun to blow, the sirocco that made the swampy areas stink like dunghills, it was decided that for sanitary reasons she be given temporary burial, keeping open the possibility, if necessary, of going on later to exhumation and autopsy.

Therefore the good women organized a collection. And everybody, more or less generously, made some contribution.

Catine had her wreath of fresh flowers, two priests, and a 'cortege' of six little girls dressed in white, a pomp and ceremony the likes of which the poor woman would never have been able to foresee.

The nuns from the hospice meanwhile had for the time being taken in Mariutine and Rosùte. Mainly to keep her occupied, they had put Mariutine into the training school. Rosùte, they would have liked to put with the tots in the nursery, but she refused to be separated from her sister.

'All right, it's just for a few days,' thought the mother superior, and she had refrained from insisting.

But at the training school, the nun who was the teacher immediately understood, half surprised, half reproachful, that, at her age, Mariutine hadn't yet learned how to hold a needle in her hand. She didn't know how to use a thimble, she broke off the sewing thread a full meter long, and she made stitches that were crooked and messy and botched like a shoemaker's. In all truth, the young girl tried hard to do her best to learn. Quick and intelligent as she was, in a brief time perhaps she might have become as adept as the others of her own age. Yes, she would have learned sewing, but, for the few days that she would be staying there, was it worth the trouble of teaching her?

Moreover, she bore another burden about which the whole hospice was profoundly scandalized. Questioned, she had candidly confessed that she had not yet made her first Communion, and, as far as religious practices were concerned, she attended church only maybe once a year.

'But on Sundays don't you go to Holy Mass?'

'We were always on the road. We went from place to place.'

'And didn't you ever step into a church?'

'Oh yes, when we were tired.'

'But what about when you were home, in your village?'

'The church was far away. Three hours through the mountains.'

All this was spoken in a rough, broken, virtually incomprehensible dialect.

'And what did you used to do, dear, when you were at home?' continued the mother superior, patient and stubborn.

'I took care of the sheep.'

'And your mother?'

'*Mâri* did everything else.'

It was not very clear what exactly this *everything else* referred to, but in the estimation of the nuns, the poor woman Catine was by now judged and condemned to the flames of hell for all eternity. She must doubtless have been a mother without conscience and without scruples, slovenly, indifferent to her offspring and to their most sacred obligations.

'Poor girls, to think that they will be going back to *such an environment*,' sighed the worried mother superior.

The story of Catine and the two orphan girls had meanwhile reached the ears of a certain lady who lived in those parts. She was a rich widow, childless, perpetually quarreling with her relatives, a bit eccentric, but very charitable. She lived in a villa surrounded by an old park, alone with the servants, two monkeys, a parrot, and innumerable cats and dogs. She was rarely seen outdoors, but when she did happen to go out, she always went to the hospice. Stout, dressed in old-fashioned magnificence, she descended upon that place in a way that inspired a great deference, and she unfailingly left a generous offering there.

Upon this good lady there flashed the idea of taking in one of the orphan girls as a *spiritual daughter*. Why not? Whether to spite her relatives or to relieve her own solitude it seemed to her a marvelous idea.

She came to town unexpectedly, early in the morning, in a carriage. She made the horses stop before they reached the town, to avoid being conspicuous, and set out rapidly on foot toward the hospice, followed by a dignified manservant who was carrying a big basket of quinces for the nuns. Five minutes later, at the café, nothing else was being talked about except this visit.

'It would be a phenomenal stroke of luck for the one who gets the chance,' someone said.

'Better if some local girl were considered,' objected another. 'Aren't there any orphans here?'

'Let's not be parochial,' rebuked a third without raising his eyes from the cards he held in his hand.

'It's your turn. Go. Ace of clubs. For my part, it would be better not to choose anyone. She'd only become a misfit.'

In the visitors' parlor, meanwhile, between the obsequious mother superior and the impatient Donna Emmelina, a mysterious conversation was taking place.

'Unfortunately nothing can be decided without the consent of the family or whoever acts in their behalf,' said the mother superior. 'It seems they no longer have a father. The older girl says that he died in America. It seems they lived, up there, with a brother of their late father's, who would be their only relative and closest kin. We expect this man to arrive any time now, for he has to come sooner or later. I will let you know right away, madam. But, by the way, what about you, Donna Emmelina, which one would you prefer? The big girl or the little one?'

'The little one,' replied Donna Emmelina without hesitation. 'I like the little girl better. I have the impression that she is more sensitive. As for me, I put feelings above all else.'

Donna Emmelina's 'impression' derived from the fact that at first sight of her Rosùte burst into tears and a gush of weeping and wailing as if she had laid eyes on the devil, but the mother superior had remarked that, poor little dear, she always carried on that way for grief over her mother's death. Mariutine, on the other hand, had held back from anything but a greeting, a smile, and whatever reply she could make to direct questions; she had let herself be observed meekly by that stout lady who scrutinized her from head to toe. Unselfconsciously the girl's expression was so alive, so direct, her face so fresh and radiant, that had she not been in mourning, with her little black flannel smock, one would surely not have been able to tell that she had been struck by so recent and grave a misfortune.

In all truth, Rosùte did seem the more affected and bereaved by Catine's death. Surely she did not comprehend what had taken place and what was meant by the word *death,* but she had suffered such a shock at seeing her mother collapse in the middle of the road, and she had remained so dreadfully upset over not having seen her any more since then, that she had cried and sobbed inconsolably for days without anyone's being able to get her to stop.

And now, she had gotten into the habit of tears even if she was not thinking about her mother. Now she cried just the way a puppy yelps, maybe also because she felt lost amid new people and new ways of doing things, disoriented by the very prosperity and orderliness that surrounded her—by the bath to which they subjected her every morning, by the disinfectant applied to her injured foot. And she was especially terrified, dreading that they would separate her from her sister.

To her sister she clung, she stuck, she was tied—from

dawn to dusk. She followed her everywhere. If her sister moved even a single step away from her, she sought her out with uneasy, anxious eyes. With infinite patience Mariutine tried to calm and reassure her. She tended her with loving care. Evenings, she cradled her in her arms, lulling and rocking her until little by little Rosùte fell asleep.

In only a few days Rosùte had wasted away. She still had her full chubby cheeks, but they were pale with an anemic pallor, and the freckles showed more distinctly on those cheeks and on her little hands, clustered thickly like a splatter of yellow dust.

'Where could poor Petòti be?' she sometimes asked her sister.

'Petòti was taken in by the king's daughter,' Mariutine answered confidently. 'They put a little bell with diamonds around his neck. He eats golden bread and silver sausage. Petòti is doing very, very well.'

No one had seen Mariutine cry for her mother. Her mother's death had been such a blow, such a treacherous, profound stab, that it had dried up and congealed even the source of her tears. Nor did she herself comprehend what she was experiencing: a chill, a freeze, something that, for her lively and exuberant nature, resembled or even equalled the sense of death. She spent the nights sleepless and dry eyed, her head hidden under the pillow of the strange cot. Grief gnawed away at her heart, grief over not having understood, over not having foreseen in time what would happen, over having let those last days pass like that without forcibly breaking her mother's terrible silence.

But no one could have guessed the girl's great suffering or what that anguish meant for a person so unsophisticated, so artless, so transparent as she was. No one would have guessed that the incapacity to express grief in any way at all, the folding in upon herself, the self-isolation were the exact measure of the depth of her grief.

The nuns and their lay assistants judged her cold and unfeeling.

Now it happened that for the celebration of the Virgin Mary's Day, which fell on September eighth, the hospice had to rehearse a choral work that on that day would be sung in the chapel by the boarding-school girls. It was a hymn to the Madonna in three stanzas, an easy, simple melody repeated three or four times, identical and monotonous.

'Do you want to sing too?' the mother superior asked Mariutine. 'Your sister said that you sing very well.'

'It's not true, Mother,' replied Mariutine, flaming up in blushes. 'I don't know how to sing.'

Unlike Rosùte, she had immediately adapted to the new life. Common sense brought her to understand at once that at the hospice she would have to find ways of making herself useful. They fed her and her sister, and it was necessary *to pay* in some way, to reciprocate for their kindness. She did not back off when confronted with hard labor, taking up the heaviest burdens and discomforts. Perhaps a subconscious need for activity and movement induced her to hurry spontaneously to where the work was hardest. Now these habits sent her to help the lay sisters wash the clothes of the sick, carry huge sacks of coal from the cellar to the laundry, hoe the vegetable garden, and clean out the toilets.

'She would be an excellent servant girl,' the nuns thought, 'if she could only be kept on.' But although the girl in no way showed it, among the sisters the impression was that she would not willingly stay with them.

Donna Emmelina meanwhile, after a long private conference, had obtained one utterly simple thing. She would take Rosùte home to her villa for that day, this being termed an experiment, the better to observe her apart from her sister, before taking on, perhaps, more serious responsibilities.

To convince Rosùte to go off with Donna Emmelina, the mother superior had had to resort to an innocent deception. She had told the child that Mariùte had gone on ahead to the lady's villa, and that by accompanying the lady she would find her there. Then Donna Emmelina put a candy in Rosùte's mouth and a big box of other candies in her hands, and this way, confused and intimidated, Rosùte had let herself be placed in the carriage beside the lady, wearing her little black frock and with the black bonnet on her head that made her resemble a mushroom.

But once she reached the villa and discovered that Mariutine was not there, she had let loose a spectacular tragedy of such howls, kicks, and scratchings that two women could hardly manage to restrain her. Donna Emmelina had to lock all the doors and assign the *gastalda* and a manservant to keep guard over her. The child was foaming at the mouth, threatening to bash her head against the walls and throw herself out of the windows. Even the parrot, the monkeys, and the dogs at her shrieks went into a frenzy, contributing to the pandemonium. The villa seemed a madhouse.

Next morning, the same carriage that had taken her away rushed Rosùte back to the hospice. Her face and eyes were swollen, her nose scratched, her new frock ripped in two places from the fury of her struggling. Every so often she gave a sudden heave on the seat of the coach, the tag end of convulsive sobbing. Donna Emmelina, who had wanted to take her back *in person*, remained seated beside her without deigning to look at her and with a face that promised nothing good.

The carriage had just turned the corner of the piazza and was heading into the narrow path to the hospice when the horses barely avoided running over a man who, in a confused manner, was roaming through the obscure lane with his nose in the air and a piece of paper in his hand, searching from door to door for the house numbers. He seemed a man who was hard up, or rather a workman, but not from around there, from somewhere else.

'Hey, my good man!' cried the driver. 'Are you blind and deaf?'

And just as the man dodged out of the way, from an alley there came darting out like a meteor a small, frightfully skinny dog the color of mud, all ruffled up as though possessed, and he hurled himself against the man with sharp yelps of joy, as though demented, leaping around and around him in frantic turns.

It was Petòti, unfortunate Petòti, abandoned since the afternoon on which Catine had taken ill on the road, Petòti who had wandered in the environs of the hospice during all the days since then seeking his mistresses, sniffing around, whining, and miraculously escaping the ambushes of the dogcatcher.

Rosùte immediately recognized both man and dog. She uttered a shriek and made as though to hurl herself from the carriage. But Donna Emmelina quickly laid hold of her by one arm, forced her back onto the seat, and did not let go of her.

'Hurry, Gioachino,' she ordered the driver. A minute later, without relaxing her grip, the lady, panting and utterly furious, entered the visitors' parlor. Rosùte had become suddenly calm.

An unusual thing, the mother superior was late.

At last she entered, solicitous, and said, 'That man we've been waiting for has just this moment arrived—the relative. Excuse me, Donna Emmelina, for the delay. If you would like to talk with him at once, to come to some agreement with him. . . . '

'For heaven's sake!' Donna Emmelina burst out, losing her temper. 'I've had enough and that's it. I wanted to bring her back personally, Mother, this little savage. From this moment every responsibility on my part is over. She drove us crazy and gave us trouble the whole night long. I give up the idea of doing her any good.'

And with that, without further explanation, she hastily said goodbye and departed without leaving any offering at all for the hospice.

✻

The man who had come to take the children away, provided with a letter from his mayor, had all his papers, all his documents in order, which certified that he was the brother of the late father of the girls, the closest living relative and having the duty and right of guardianship over the minor children. No, there was no more to be said, and, at bottom, there was consensus among the nuns as well as among the board of directors of the hospice; they all welcomed his arrival with a sense of relief. As for expenses, the accounts could be easily settled with the bookkeeper. The children meanwhile could be entrusted to him; and also entrusted to him was a residual little sum of money from the collection taken up for Catine's funeral rites, and another little hoard saved from the sale of the cart and the wooden items that the good women of the region had bought at padded 'love cost' prices, that is, by way of charitable donations. In all, it was nearly three hundred lire. At this the man had seemed satisfied enough. He had been only moderately interested in Catine's illness and death.

As for the rest, in the few hours that he had remained at the hospice, he had said in all possibly fifty words. He expressed himself more intelligibly than the children, however, in a dialect less harsh. He had been out in the world; with his late brother he had been a laborer in America, in Switzerland, and in France.

He was a redheaded man, his face covered with freckles, his appearance a bit obtuse. A scar cut his eyebrow and the eyelid of one eye, forcing him to squint in such a way that he seemed always to be laughing. A souvenir of

America, he had said, from an evening when he had had a bit much to drink. On that occasion, unfortunately for him, he lost a fight and took a beating. Since he was the victim, however, his court record was still clean.

The children called him Barbe Zef, Uncle Joe. He seemed a good man, and, what was more important, not at all bothered at having to go home with two dependents not his own to support. His livelihood was selling coal up in the mountains beneath the Mauria Pass.

Although awkward in their new clothes, new shoes, and especially those bonnets which they had to put on in order not to slight the feelings of the women who had donated them, Mariutine and Rosùte seemed eager to leave, as though freed from a nightmare, released from a chain.

A bit offended by such indifference and ingratitude, the nuns nevertheless did their duty straight to the end. They repeated fervent recommendations to Mariutine, particularly with regard to religious observances. To each of the girls they presented a prayerbook and a fine holy image, a reproduction of the dear Madonna of their own chapel. To Mariutine they also gave a bundle containing poor Catine's garments. Right after noon, the group hastily embarked on the first possible train and went away.

✳

It was a small train that climbed the mountain gasping shaking and puffing. Except during the summer, it hardly ever carried either goods or passengers, but it stopped all the same at all the stations along the way throwing off harrowing whistles and dense clouds of smoke.

After a bit, Rosùte dozed off in her sister's arms, and the man also fell asleep, with his cap over his eyes and his mouth half open, snoring intermittently. Petòti, who had come across the group as it was leaving the hospice, had resumed his place in the family with total naturalness. He was crouched under the bench, out of foot range, next to the little black bundle of Catine's clothes.

Tired and spent, Mariutine looked out of the window without thinking of anything in particular. Only from time to time she put a hand on Rosùte's hurt foot, which felt burning hot to her touch.

Several stations passed without anyone's getting on and entering their compartment. Between Perarolo and Pieve, the man interrupted his sleep to draw out of his pockets some bread and salami, which he shared with the girls. Then he went to sleep again.

At Pieve, when the train was already starting to move, a blond youth of about twenty, who had come running at top speed, flung open the train door and climbed up. He was bare headed and out of breath. With a big multicolored handkerchief he wiped the sweat from his face and from his short curly hair. Then he sat down with a sigh of relief.

Yet hardly a moment after he had taken his place, he got up again, uneasily searching here and there about his person and all around him for something he could not find. Then he turned out the contents of his pockets into his handkerchief, reviewing with great attention a *britola* or pocketknife, a small yellow leather change purse, a whistle, a piece of rope, an orange, but without finding whatever he was looking for. At last, he discovered on the floor—almost under the sleeping man's feet—a small, red, dusty rectangle. Bending down swiftly, he picked it up.

'I thought I had lost my return ticket,' he exclaimed, overcome by the need to show his joy. In saying this, he let the glance of his merry, childlike eyes rest on Mariutine, and he recognized her.

'*Mandi,* good day, Mariûte,' he exclaimed gaily. 'Don't you know me? I'm Pieri from Forni, don't you remember? The one who came around to your place so many times for coal.'

Mariutine had recognized him some time back but,

gripped by a sudden unease, she had sought to avoid his greeting. Now he would be asking about her mother, and how the misfortune had happened, and where, and when, and she would have to tell it. . . .

But instead the youth asked neither this nor that. Either he knew nothing or he had forgotten. Completely caught up in the excitement of his run and the joy of having caught the train and found his missing ticket, satisfied to have met folks he knew, he cheerfully began to tell about the events of his journey.

He had had to go down to Perarolo that day to request certain documents needed for his departure for America, Perarolo being his birthplace. He had left home before dawn and set out on his way, and at Calalzo he had taken the first train. At Perarolo, he had had to wait for the documents, worry for a long time, then turn around and run like a hare to pay his respects to all the relatives, since his mother had so strongly urged him not to forget any one of them—four aunts with their respective families, all of whom wanted him to eat and drink.

'It's a miracle that I'm still alive,' he said, laughing.

But only his feet were hurting him, pinched by those hard new shoes. And, in his race to catch the train, his hat had flown off his head—a fine hat that had cost him fourteen lire. A pity. He could not wait to get home.

'But it's a good long trip yet,' he said, 'and you have an even longer one than I do. From Calalzo to Passo . . . and then the rest of it.'

'Do you have a sure job in America?' interrupted the man, suddenly opening his good eye for an instant, and at once closing it again. 'Either a sure job or sure misery.'

'It's all set, absolutely sure,' replied the youth. 'A cousin who's like a brother is sending for me. He's been in Argentina for ten years and owns a small store. He has his family with him and they're doing well. Really well,' he repeated, looking all about him. All his words and the very expression of his naive and open countenance emanated trust and satisfaction.

'And you,' he said to Mariutine politely, 'has business been good?'

'So-so . . . ' murmured the girl, turning her eyes away.

Meanwhile the youth had spread the colored handkerchief over his knees in order not to soil his holiday suit, and with close attention he began peeling the orange.

'If you please, . . . ' he said, offering half of it to Mariutine.

'That's too much,' the girl declined. 'One section would be enough.'

Only then did he seem to notice her aloofness, and her strange manner, and her black dress, and how changed she was from the merry singing Mariutine he remembered. Suddenly there returned to his mind talk he had heard about something—yes, a misfortune—and he was swept by a sense of embarrassment.

For a bit he cast about for a way to change the conversation so as to make up for his blunder and forgetfulness, but he did not find one. Mariutine had leaned her head against the wall and she was sleeping or pretending to sleep, and he kept silent and watched her with a mortified expression in his candid eyes.

The train, nearing Calalzo, had begun to whistle desperately. That was the last station. Everybody had to get off to take the mountain road.

Mariutine gently and gradually roused Rosùte, sat her on the bench, and began to gather up the bundles. They had very peculiar shapes, those several bundles—long and narrow, wrapped in old newspapers and held together by a ribbon; a pair of cloth slippers within the knotted corners of a kerchief, a humped and knobby sack with its neck end tied by a string, a kettle and some other kitchen implements in a lightweight woolen blanket.

The man hoisted to his shoulder the sack and the biggest bundles, threading them along a walking stick.

'My foot hurts,' whimpered Rosùte, rubbing her eyes.

Mariutine knelt down beside her and unlaced one shoe. 'Where does it hurt? Here? . . . Here? . . . Now it'll go away.' And taking the little foot between her hands, she kissed it.

'Calalzo!' shouted a voice running along the train behind the wavering light of a lantern. 'Calalzo! Calalzo!'

With a great noise of clanking iron, the train came to a stop.

'This *frute,* this little girl doesn't walk,' said the youth, nodding at the child. 'Give her to me to carry. You have enough other stuff to handle.'

He sat the child on his shoulders and was about to dismount, when he noticed that there had remained behind in a corner of the compartment the two black bonnets, which Mariutine and Rosùte had taken off with relief once out of sight of their donors.

'And what about those, what do we do with them? Leave them?' asked Pieri. 'I, truly, could really use a good cooking pot,' he exclaimed. And despite his intention to remain serious and dignified in keeping with the circumstances, he grasped one of the bonnets with his free hand and clamped it onto his head down to his ears and burst out laughing, while for the first time, looking at him, Mariutine and Rosùte also laughed.

'Leave them where they are,' said Mariutine. 'So much for them, they're no more use to us.'

＊

The road that winds from Calalzo in the direction of the Mauria Pass crosses through a rich area of towns and settlements, varied and undulating terrain, very beautiful, between darkly wooded mountains.

Once outside the station, the little group set off quickly for the road that stretched out in the middle of broad meadows in a gradual ascent toward the east. It was neither day nor evening, but rather that moment when the light, still and as though suspended over all the outspread world, gives the landscape a sense of waiting, an indefinite, fluid, almost unreal appearance. A light mist rose up from the meadows, softening and blurring the outlines of the houses, the woods, and the mountains. The pointed roof of a bell tower here and there, nearby, distant, gleamed as though made of silver.

But the travelers had hardly left the road to take the shortcut that narrowed between the mountains when night fell at one fast and sudden swoop.

It was a moonless night, and one could not see ten steps ahead. Nevertheless the man with his sack humped on his back, Mariutine loaded down with bundles, and the cheery youth with the little girl on his shoulders set out on their hike without hesitation. They moved ahead in single file, with an even gait and the sure instinct that allows mountain people to distinguish the right path even blindfolded, recognizing it by the scent of the grass, the sponginess of the ground, the shape of a certain rock, yet knowing quite well that with the mountain one doesn't take chances.

Petòti, excited and happy, ran back and forth, traversing a stretch of road three or four times, going on ahead of his master and mistresses and turning to race back again to look for them when he could no longer see them, loitering to sniff around here and there or to pee against the rocks, disappearing at one moment to reappear unexpectedly higher up, emerging from who knows where, waiting patiently with his tongue hanging out.

And little by little the travelers' eyes, accustomed to the darkness, made out here and there on the higher slopes the sleeping cheese factories, the sawmills, the huts, the haystacks, the signs of the flocks that had been passing through. Occasionally some shepherd's dog, on guard over an alpine pasture, rushed forth barking furiously, whereupon Pieri pretended to pick up a stone and throw it at him, while Petòti padded hastily away to take cover quietly behind Mariutine's skirts.

Above the spacious clearings of the pastures the line of the woods appeared and followed like a shadow, an interminable dark streak beneath the colorless sky. The path ran from one to another height in a succession of rises and descents that looked as though they would never end, now overhanging a gorge narrow like a corridor, now crossing small damp meadows where a thread of water flowed almost on top of the ground, flooding the grass engorged and mushy like a sponge.

Gradually, as the ascent became steeper, the mountain stood out more bare and rugged. It became violent and more naked, with its tufts of scanty grass, its deformed crags toppled in rockslides down the slopes, its peaks cold, sharp, cutting, against the sky. And there in the depth of the valley, as though all lit at once at a single stroke, were the lights of Calalzo, Pieve, and Domegge: vivid, lightly twinkling like eyes full of laughter.

'See?' said the youth to Rosùte, who had immediately trusted him. 'You see that long line of burning lights? . . . It's Calalzo, where we stopped. And that sort of colored wreath? It's the big hotel of Pieve.'

Suddenly they saw nothing more. At a sharp bend of the mule track, as though swallowed up by the mountain, they turned their backs on places where people dwelt and they were completely immersed in shadow.

For a long stretch they encountered neither cheese factories nor huts. Seen from behind, the man going ahead of the others, with his hump of a sack on his back, took on the strange and grotesque outlines of a nocturnal monster. Mariutine was walking behind him silently and now even Pieri kept quiet, overcome by sudden sleepiness against which he was hard pressed to keep his eyes open. His shoes hurt his feet. Rosùte surrendered herself on his back like a dead weight, and he would have liked to set her down on the ground for a moment at least so that he could sit down on a rock to rest—darn it! he had a right to that, he'd been up since dawn!—but a sense of pride and childish bravado kept him from doing so. Had he been alone, he would certainly have sat down for a good half hour, but he was ashamed in front of Mariutine, and for nothing in the world would he have confessed an inability to go on, while she, nothing but a girl, that *fantate*, kept on walking unperturbed without giving a sign of fatigue.

All along the way, Mariutine had never addressed a word to him, not even to thank him for having picked up and carried her sister—and this seemed unfair to him. Not even one word. Yet it was hardly a negligible effort to go up the mountain with that weight on one's shoulders. It was like carrying two big sheep. Not everybody would have had his strength.

'She must be offended because I didn't ask about her *mâri*, her mamma . . . ' thought the wondering youth. And he quickened his steps to draw up even with the girl and to try to open a conversation. But she, with her big bundles, took up the whole width of the path and walked without turning around. Pieri could not manage to see even her profile. He saw only the blond braids that went on ahead of him in the darkness.

'We have already come about two-thirds of the way,' he consoled himself. And then he thought that at home he would certainly find his mother still up and waiting for him and that she would have fixed him something good to eat. This thought cheered him. It almost made him forget his tiredness, but he didn't dare speak—not even about the treats his mother would have ready for him—out of respect for that other mother who was dead. He was afraid of committing further blunders. Mariutine's silence greatly embarrassed him.

'Strange,' he said at one point without realizing he was speaking aloud, 'it seemed to me that I had eaten plenty at

Perarolo, and now my stomach feels empty, yes, absolutely empty.'

'Me too,' announced Rosùte, waking up appropriately for this discovery.

And just then Petòti suddenly stopped in his tracks and began to bark. From above, some loose stones came rolling down along the ravines. The little group halted to listen. The man sharpened his eyes but could not see anything. He gave a whistle.

'Uhiiih!'

And from high above, in the nocturnal silence, a whistle answered back: 'Uhiiih!'

Now the wanderer could be discerned. A small grey blot the color of the rocks: it had to be a *bocia,* a 'boy,' one of those young fellows whom shepherds of the alpine grazing grounds pay to mind the flocks during pasture season. And he was coming down leaping like a chamois from rock to rock first on one side of the gully and then the other. If he was out and about in the mountains at that time of night, it had to be because of some trouble.

In fact, as soon as he was within speaking distance, the fellow stopped and, shielding his face with his hands around his mouth, he shouted, gasping for breath, 'The master's gone down to the plain with the flock and left us there, my brother and me, in charge of the grazing ground with a cow that can't walk. Now the cow is sick, she's so sick, I'm afraid she'll die on me before the master returns.'

He was a boy of thirteen or fourteen, scared, and he began to cry.

'Where do you come from?' asked the man.

'The Case Rotte.'

'Who is your master?'

'Compare Àgnul.'

'Wait for me. I'm coming now.'

The Case Rotte were a group of buildings on a broad plateau. There were three or four dilapidated cheese factories of stone and wood in the middle of large enclosures. In the pasturing season the alpine grazing ground attracted a diverse and unruly population: a hundred assorted animals, counting cows, sheep, and dogs, with their respective keepers. But now that the flocks had left the high mountain to descend down below, the Case Rotte appeared completely deserted, except for the one lowest down, where a tiny lit-up window glowed.

From far away that light seemed clear and bright like a star, but in reality it came only from a wavering and smoky oil lamp attached by a hook to a beam of the stable. The stable, serving as infirmary, was small and low, with a floor all full of holes, rough walls that seemed smeared with mud, and black beams from which were hanging large spiderwebs. And in the stable was a single cow, skinny, with a big belly and drooping ears, and beside her a very small and terribly sleepy boy wearing a large, green wool stocking cap. In a cage hanging from the wall, a little bird was sleeping curled up on itself in a little ball, its head beneath its wing.

'What kind of a birdie is it?' asked Rosùte in a whisper, tugging at Pieri's jacket.

'It looks like a *franzèl,* a finch,' replied Pieri. 'Is it blind?' he asked the herd boy in turn, with this question addressing him for the first time in an elderly and authoritative tone.

The fellow barely indicated his assent with a nod, while his lively black eyes fixed worriedly on Barbe Zef, who had entered the cow's resting place.

Barbe Zef scratched his head, understanding at a glance what was the matter. Calving had begun prematurely, and though the animal was having a hard time it was not a desperate case. The boy had panicked too quickly. He himself was experienced in those affairs. On this occasion he had arrived barely in time to save the cow—but maybe he could save the calf, too.

He cast the sack and the bundles behind a manger and rolled up his sleeves. Pieri and the two herd boys, ready at his commands, followed his movements with keen attention. For a while he maneuvered around the cow, but without result. Then swiftly he made up his mind. 'Let's go,' he ordered, laying hold of the baby calf's feet. 'Let's go, boys!'

Pieri and the herd boy, holding on to the belt of his trousers like sailors at their ropes, also pulled with as much energy as they had in their bodies.

Mariutine had gone on into the kitchen and, assisted by the smaller boy, had hastily lit the fire in order to prepare hot water. When she returned to the stable she carried a large steaming bucket. Setting it in a corner, she sat down out of the way with Rosùte, patiently and indifferently waiting until the business should be over.

After a few minutes a little creature with grey slimy skin, a dark snout, and long unsteady legs was crouched beside the cow, who began to lick it while lowing and moaning.

'A fine little calf, a fine little calf,' murmured the satisfied man. 'Boy, prepare its bed, because now it has to be moved away from the mother.'

'I know,' said the boy with a self-important manner, and having taken up the hayfork, he hurried to spread dry grass evenly in the small, low section reserved for the calves. From time to time he cast oblique glances at Pieri, who in turn was watching him work, his hands in his pockets and a slight mocking smirk on his face.

Mariutine had taken down the oil lamp from its hook and lit up the scene. The man took the newborn animal in his arms as though it were a baby and laid it very gently in its bed, while the cow, its lowing immediately ended, slowly turned her head toward him, gazing with sad eyes.

All had gone well and there was no more to be done. The herd boy was satisfied yet at the same time worried, fearing the man would want to be paid for his services. But the man asked for nothing. He wiped his hands with a fistful of leaves, gave some further instructions to the boy, and having gathered up his possessions again, he started for the door. Only on the threshold, before going out he asked, 'Might you by any chance have a drop of grappa? I'm all sweaty.'

The herd boy rushed into the kitchen and came right back with a tiny flask of dark glass.

'It's not much,' he murmured all red faced and ashamed.

'Good enough as it is,' asserted the man, drinking avidly and wiping his mouth with the back of his hand. 'Tell him, tell your boss, when he comes back,' he added, 'that it was Zef, the coalman from Bosco Tagliato, who delivered his cow. He knows me. Had I not been here, tomorrow on his return, instead of a cow and a calf, he'd have found two discarded hides to tan.'

And he laughed good naturedly, or it seemed that he laughed, with his eye half open and half closed.

∗

The brief stop and diversion had distracted and revived them all. In the cage hung from the stable wall the blind finch, roused by the voices, began to chirp, believing that daylight had come, and it too seemed pleased with the calf's birth.

Once outdoors, Rosùte claimed her foot no longer hurt and she could now walk. She didn't want Pieri to get any more tired on account of carrying her.

'I get tired, I?' the youth protested. 'But I could carry you as far as Sappada or Comeglians. I have the strength to run up the slopes for hours with any kind of weight whatever on my back. One time a calf of ours fell into a ravine and broke a leg, and I climbed down to retrieve it, and then I carried it from Malga Petrosa, you know where that is, all the way to my house, just that way, for five hours' walking distance. A calf almost as big as an ox, or rather even bigger than an ox. It didn't bother me in the least. Don't you believe me? Anyway it's true.'

But Rosùte by no means doubted it. She had taken hold of Pieri's hand, and watched him and listened to him with great admiration.

'They must be real dummies,' Pieri continued with a disdainful air, 'to start crying and run out like that at night because a cow is having a hard time. At my house I'm the one who looks after the animals and nothing like that ever happened to me. I have a mule, four cows, a pig, and twelve sheep. Does that seem little to you? I manage them all by myself. My mother doesn't even know that they're around.'

'Such accidents can always happen,' retorted the man authoritatively.

'Sure, Barbe, but one needn't lose heart. With courage everything can be done. Looking after animals, however, isn't the kind of job that would suit me for the rest of my life.'

By now they had reached the spot where they had to go their separate ways. The youth had to turn a bit eastward and had scarcely half an hour's walk ahead of him before reaching his grazing ground. The others had to go still further up to reach the Mauria Pass, and then onward from there.

A bleak sharp wind had started up. Several times in succession, nearby and then still nearer, the cry of a noc-turnal bird reverberated.

'The owls of Bosco Tagliato . . . ' said Pieri. 'You too are near home.'

The goodbyes were rapid. At least at the moment of leave-taking, Pieri would have liked to find something to say about the 'misfortune,' but he did not know how to start on the subject.

'Before going overseas, I just may stop by to give my

regards,' was all he managed to promise, suddenly serious, looking straight at Mariutine.

'Yes, come, come!' exclaimed Rosùte.

'*Mandi,* Rosùte! Give me your hand! *Mandi,* Mariùte! *Mandi! Mandi!*'

And exchanging handshakes with all three, the youth set off in haste without looking back, his red kerchief tied around his neck and his blond hair ruffled by the wind.

*

To reach their small farmhouse, the three had to cross over the most desolate area of the mountain. There, where formerly had been a thick woods, the trees had been cut down, and the long slender and straight trunks of the pines thrown down the slope and abandoned to the rushing stream that had borne them to the plain below. On poor and yellowish ground, where for years and years the sun had never managed to shine its rays, the stumps of the trees remained, sawed off at a short height from the ground, similar to enormous stumps of human limbs nailed to the earth. Rains, winds, and snows had torn away the bark from these stumps, and emptied them of their sap, and they now appeared naked, grey, and more like bone than wood, without a green leaf, without shadow of life. Nothing was left as a reminder of the freshness and sweetness of the living tree.

In the evening, the sinister stand of stumps seemed like a troupe of deformed dwarves emerging chest high out of the earth, motionless, yet as if tormented by a tragic wind. By day, the site was squalid, with a melancholy and barren squalor, unprotected and horribly battered by sun or rain. But for the girls and the man, accustomed as they were to the stark shapes of the mountain, that spectacle represented nothing unusual. For the eldest and for the youngest, it signified only the end of the journey, the safe and near place where they could find shelter. For Mariutine, it signified the unexpected reawakening of something that

43

had seemed petrified and shut in forever, the rapid beating of her heart at the return of an image long invoked in vain.

She thought that she had left her poor *mâri* far away, behind her forever, alone there below under a cross in the alien cemetery, and never, never, not even in the first days after her death, not even when she called her throughout entire nights in her cot at the hospice, for however long she might have sought her, never had she succeeded in summoning back her face or her eyes, or hearing within herself that beloved voice, or seeing her again as she had been when alive.

And now, behold, without having called her up, her mother was coming to meet her: *she,* as she had remained in memory unconsciously from the days of childhood: lithe and erect, with shining dark hair, carrying baby Rosùte in her arms. She was coming forward among the stumps in silence, and she was looking at Mariutine. The sheep were grazing on the short grass all around. . . . Then later . . . when? . . . Maybe there was a gap of years between the one and the other vision. *She* is seated over there on that trunk just recently felled that tomorrow will be given up to the rushing stream: already with her hair not so dark, already bent and sad. . . . She has placed on the ground the bag with the lunch for Barbe Zef, who will come down from the woods at midday. She is waiting. Then still more. . . . The *mâri* of the last days, pale and drawn, with the kerchief tied under her chin like an old woman. . . . She comes down from the mountain, cross-ing through the stand of stumps with the heavy bag on her shoulders, she goes slowly towards home . . . as though she were dragging her poor tired feet, swollen and deformed . . . A paroxysm of coughing. . . .

'Mariutine!' calls a voice in the silence, 'Mariutine! . . .'

Nothing has changed in this place for years. Nothing will change for years and years to come.

In cities, villages, and other populated areas, life

changes and flows. The appearance of things can be transformed from one month to the next. Man constructs houses, suspends bridges, builds roads; man erects and tears down; people leave and new people replace them; impressions overlay impressions. But the rhythm of mountain life is so slow and even that to the human eye images are transfixed in marble immobility. Mariutine knows that she will be able to go, to come back, to stay away half her lifetime, and upon her return find everything unchanged.

Once she did not like that state of affairs. On returning from the plain, from the prospering and busy countryside, she used to feel a tightening of her heart at seeing the barren grey peaks of the mountains again. When she was able to prolong her trip, once upon a time, she would lead her flock to pasture in the direction of the valley where at least from high up, when the air was clear, she saw rise up from afar a plume of smoke or there reached her—not always, but when the wind was right—the cry of a child, the snarl of a dog—evidence of the presence of living beings.

Or the mountain stream attracted her because it was live and eccentric and always new. One day it was all dried stones tormented in their wild bed, the next it was rapid and cheerful between high banks fragrant with mint; another day yet, it became swollen turbid and plundering.

When the stream was swollen and the water rushed down, Mariutine would feel a giddy exhilaration. She sang out then with open throat, and, who knows, it seemed to her she was no longer alone with her flock on the mountain, and that the water carried her pretty folk songs away to someone: to whom, she did not know, to distant houses, to villages, to people, to someone who would respond to them. And meanwhile she was her own audience, inventing songs, making up questions and responses, hurling into the water handfuls of mint she pulled out here and there and that her gaze followed while they fled eddying and swirling.

But the sinister desolation of Bosco Tagliato once upon a time had horrified her. There no leafy branch rustled, and there was no fluttering of wings. Roots of the dead trees emerged from the earth like enormous tentacles. Sole inhabitants by day, enormous reddish ants made their perpetual comings and goings along the deformed stumps. By night, as in cemeteries, yellow-eyed owls perched from trunk to trunk, emitting all around them lugubrious cries. And, by a mysterious instinct, even the flock, when towards evening it was forced to cross over the sinister expanse of cut stumps, seemed afraid of it. The sheep halted all together, nudging one another with lowered snouts, and Mariutine and Petòti had a hard time getting them to move on. Finally they moved in great haste, and behind them the dog and the girl themselves ran without looking back, as though pursued by the devil.

Once. But now . . . now from that very place, sorrowful and inhuman, and from her very own desolate immobility, there came over her instead a sense of comfort, of security. The dreadful emptiness of boundless solitude was no longer there: the mother filled it with her breath. Elsewhere she, Mariutine, had called in vain; here, *she* had come towards her. All nature had her eyes, sad and deep; silence speaks with her voice. Here nothing will change. . . . Here the mother will exist eternally. . . . She used to walk bent over, evading direct glances—*suffering*—Mariutine remembers!—wherever she was obliged to walk among and associate with people. Only dire need, only that, forced her with her little cart through the roads of the world. Here no one will disturb her, no human glance will make her suffer. . . . Only here, only here, will she be truly at peace! . . .

And finally Mariutine's heart melts, finally tears well forth freely from her eyes while she turns back, repeatedly, toward the area of stumps she is leaving behind her. Rosùte luckily does not know she is crying. She is so tired that she walks with eyes shut. But maybe she understands and keeps quiet; she drags along her helpless foot without asking to be carried.

All around, huge naked mounds rear up in a silence incomparable to any other silence.

Tomorrow the long winter, the deep snow. . . .

PART TWO

*T*he Zef family's cabin was in a little valley fairly well protected from the winds by a cliff. Theirs was one of the usual high mountain huts whose poverty and primitiveness are hard to imagine sight unseen, its lower part made up of a plaster wall, its upper part of spruce trunks laid sideways, and its roof pointed and projecting. It consisted of one bedroom and a kitchen, above which was the hayloft. Beside it stood the sheepfold, which could shelter only a few sheep, and contained a windowless storeroom where Barbe Zef kept his coal and tools. In the storeroom was also a ladder where two or three hens roosted. To prevent the piercing cold of the long winters from entering, the windows of this dwelling were ever so small, and they were rarely opened in any season at all. Into the sealed interior of the house even light hardly penetrated.

While Catine was alive, she and the little girls usually slept together in the only bed, which was high and narrow and had a creaking mattress filled with dry leaves. Barbe Zef had slept in the storeroom on a straw pallet arranged as well as possible upon two planks. But, during the women's annual trip, invariably he took over the main room and the big bed, and on their return it took a lot of persuading to make him clear out. Every year it was the same story.

'Isn't there room enough for everybody?' he grumbled. 'Aren't you taking over the whole place? Out there it's damp; it's not fit for dogs; I've got pains; and furthermore I get full of those lice from the hens.' But Catine was unyielding. She did not open her mouth; rather, she took the man's stuff up in her arms and carried it out and then she slammed the door sharply.

Once, when Mariutine was nine or ten years old, a scene had occurred that made a deep impression on her. Returning from their journey, they had found Barbe Zef utterly drunk. Unfortunately this occurred frequently, and that evening, although Catine as usual had plunked his stuff where she thought it belonged, he had not gone along with that. He had cursed, sneered, and made long speeches with neither head nor tail to them, chasing after Catine with his arms stretched out, his red hair disheveled and eyes blurry. Finally, to prevent her from shutting him out, he sat down across the threshold of her bedroom, declaring that from there he would not be budged.

That time too Catine had said nothing. She had continued to come and go about her business with her lips tightly compressed, nor did she look at the man, as though he were a chair or a stone, dodging however, when he, stumbling, seemed about to fall upon her. But finally, when she was through with the housework, she had gone directly toward him and had caught hold of him by one arm.

'Get out,' she had said without raising her voice, but glaring at him full in the face with her opaque, sad, cold eyes that froze one's blood just looking at them. 'Get out of here, you filthy slob!'

Mariutine expected a terrible scene, for when he was drunk Barbe Zef could become violent. Instead, he had immediately quit every notion of rebellion. He had gotten up staggering with his back hunched and gone away.

Mariutine had felt sorry for him. Of course the bed was not all that big, but squeezing themselves a bit, it could have served well enough for four. At bottom, it had seemed to the girl that in that circumstance her mother had been very harsh with Barbe Zef. Petòti, a dog, was permitted to sleep with them, but not the master of the house? . . . This seemed an injustice. If not in the bed, why not at least allow him to stay in the room?

Barbe Zef was not a bad man; Mariutine did not recall ever having received either a mean word or a blow from him. He was hard working. Up and about before dawn, he went out and did not return until nighttime, whether it was to cut firewood in the woods or to look after his pile of coal, for the Zef family from father to son had all been coal men. Although with coal coming from Yugoslavia this employment now earned him little or nothing, upon his return from America he had not wanted to wrack his brains looking for another type of work.

Week after week he went down to the villages with the sack on his back and made his rounds from house to house to sell the coal. And he tried making a living in so many other ways, too. The farmers of the cheese factories half-way up the mountain called him for their pigstickings, butchering, and sausage making, and the shepherds for advice when there were signs of an epidemic in the herd or when a cow was having a hard time calving. Of the little money that he scraped together this way, spending hours and hours on the road, he brought home the entire sum. They were mainly just a few coins. Other times, though, he came back drunk, swearing and cursing that he had lost them.

✳

Yes, drinking was his weakness, and when he was drunk he became utterly transformed. With a strange twisted face, he was whimpering, quarrelsome, or of an immoder-ate cheerfulness—and talkative and petulant, he, who usually did not utter more than ten words in a whole day. While they were just little tots, the girls had been amused by the show. Then, as they grew older, they ended up running away from him at those ugly moments, almost ashamed for him. After a few hours of drunkenness and a good sleep, however, he would come back to his former self and get down to work again. He didn't expect anything, being satisfied with a little food and some cold water. And he would come back from the woods with mushrooms or with strawberries, according to the season, and if he went to draw and quarter a pig somewhere, he would bring back in his knapsack a hunk of salted lard.

The girls forgot his drunken binges quickly and sought him out again. Though he might have a blackened face and hands, seeing him made them cheerful, for even if he didn't laugh, on account of his damaged eye he always seemed to be laughing and to be in a good mood, and the good eye, if one knew how to look at it, was cunning and bright.

✳

But, whether Barbe Zef were drunk or sober, the girls' mother seemed to hate him. It was impossible to know why. His very presence aggravated her morose and almost anguished disposition. She never said good morning or good evening to him. She never even looked him in the face. She brought him his meals and washed and patched his trousers, but that was all. When the girls ran to him, she called them back angrily.

'Frutes!'—girls!—she cried, and she did not relax unless they held on to her apron strings.

Nevertheless they had stayed together since ever so long ago, since forever, from when their father had died and even before that, maybe. Mariutine did not really know, she didn't remember. Her mother never spoke about those things. Mariutine knew only that her father, Gaspari Zef, and her uncle, Giuseppe Zef, brothers, had gone together to America when she was a tot and that from there Barbe had returned alone because her father was dead. Moreover, in America Barbe had, besides a dead brother, a live wife, whom he had married there and whom they had never seen. She was a woman of those *foreign* parts, who had not wanted to come to Italy with him and had not given any further sign of her existence.

✳

Barbe Zef set his sack down on the ground and drew out of his pocket an oversized rusted key that he turned with great effort in the lock. The cabin door opened and precisely at that moment there again flashed on Mariutine the memory of that whole business about the room and the bed. Beforehand she had not thought about it, and she felt gripped by a keen anxiety. Fixed in her memory remained her mother's implacable resistance.

'The *mâri* didn't want this,' she told herself. But she felt diffident, weak, a child incapable of refusing to obey if Barbe Zef ordered her. 'My god. . . . The *mâri* didn't want . . . ' If her uncle insisted, what should she do? . . . Her mother had dealt with him as an equal, but she, how would she be able to do that? . . . He was the boss, now. Truly, he had been that before too, since Mariutine was quite sure, although no one had ever told her, that her late father had spent his entire portion of the inheritance and so had no further right to the pasture and the flock. Barbe Zef must then have kept them out of charity, and now that the *mâri* was no longer there, if he got fed up, he could send them away from one moment to the next. Rosùte perhaps not, for she was too young and small, but she herself he could send away as a servant in some shepherd's grazing place, far off and separated from her sister. This worrisome thought made her heart beat hard with fear.

'But I am not staying here out of charity; I'm earning my own way. I'm earning my daily bread, for me and for my *frutes!*' Catine had said one day.

When had it been? . . . Mariutine could recall neither the occasion nor the reason; she could recall only the tone of her mother's voice, that rough, hard tone that it had taken on in the last years. When was it? . . . One of the rare times that she had opened her mouth to say something. . . .

Ah, however it may have been, her uncle did seem to be afraid of or dominated by their mother. But what of her, a young girl of fourteen? . . . How would she ever dare to chase him out as her mother had chased him? . . . Now that the *mâri* was no longer there, everything was utterly different!

While Barbe Zef was lighting the little oil lamp—the matches were damp and he had a hard time getting them to light—the young girl avoided even looking at him. She sought to make as little noise as possible, to postpone making a decision, rummaging among the bundles and loitering in the kitchen.

But Rosùte was sleepy and tugged at her sister's skirt. 'What are you doing? Why are you staying out here? Let's go to bed,' she whimpered.

Luckily Barbe went straight to his storeroom. Mariutine heard him while he was moving around out there, preparing his pallet, throwing his sack to the ground amid the frightened, wing-flapping hens and cursing between his teeth as was his wont when irritated or dissatisfied. But this lasted hardly a few minutes, and soon afterwards his deep snoring reached her ears.

✳

Before Mariutine untied her shoes, Rosùte had climbed onto the bed and fallen asleep fully clothed. Mariutine covered her as best she could. Truly she did not regret missing the chance to tuck her in underneath, for the sheets on the bed—and they were the only pair they possessed—had been on the bed since they had gone away and, Barbe Zef having slept there, were as black as his coal pile.

'Tomorrow I'll wash them in the stream. If the weather's good, they'll dry in a few hours,' she told herself, and she leaned over to look at her little sister's pale and chubby face on which the long eyelashes cast a light shadow. Rosùte slept stretched out on her back with her lips parted. Her red hair, in the wavering light of the little oil lamp, appeared limp as though soaked. Her freckled little hands lay opened out on the coverlet and from time to time they twitched as through a reflex action.

Placed with two sides up against the wall, the very high bed took up almost the entire room and almost touched the little door giving entrance to the sheepfold. From the other side the great wooden chest appeared black against the wall, the one that had been Catine's wedding chest. Her crudely carved initials, C. M. Z., still stood out clearly on the dark wood. Besides that there was nothing except a chair with half its straw bottom missing and a squash lying on the sill of the tiny window.

Mariutine lightly touched Rosùte's forehead. Burning? . . . Bearing the lamp high with one hand, with the other she cautiously uncovered the injured foot and inspected it. It looked swollen and a bit red. The nuns had recommended applying disinfectant daily.

'Where did I put the iodine? . . . This foot that doesn't heal . . . I'll have to take care of it tomorrow. . . .' thought the girl. 'It's cold here . . . ' and she undid the bundle of Catine's clothes, drew out an old, threadbare shirt full of patches, and spread it out lightly over the sleeping child's legs. 'Poor *frute!* . . . ' she murmured, caught up in a new flood of emotion.

The tears she had lately wept had left her vulnerable to crying even more. She had been unable to cry before and that had made her suffer even more sharply; now the tears were teeming forth like a stream spurting from a spring. She could not stop them. Had she been able at least to curl up there in the darkness, on the worn-out steps, and, without anyone knowing it, to cry and cry until she were all cried out . . .

But Rosùte threw off the cover. She was breathing fitfully, uttering a little moan. Once so chubby and placid, she had become nervous after her mother's death. She got scared and upset over nothing. It did not do for Mariutine to let herself be seen crying!

Mariutine was not sleepy. She felt herself in the grip rather of that almost feverish excitation that accompanies profound weariness. To avoid making noise she took off her shoes, moving around like a soul in torment in the narrow unoccupied space. In front of the chest, she stopped for an instant and mechanically raised and lowered its lid. A black scorpion scurried rapidly out. Now Mariutine's eyes wandered uneasily along the walls and in the cracks of the floor. Where had it gone, that scorpion? . . . Let it not sting Rosùte while she slept. . . . She bent down to peer under the bed: dust and cobwebs; and a little heap of half-rotted potatoes . . . What a mess, what a stench of dankness, and what a disgusting smell in that ugly room!

On the ground, between the tiny window and the bed was a bundle of rags—the *pieces* of Barbe Zef, those pieces of clothing that the *mâri* took hold of with her fingertips and threw contemptuously into the water separately from their stuff, maybe because, had they been washed together, they would have stained everything black. Tomorrow she would have to throw open doors and windows, carry every single thing outside, and kill off the scorpions. And maybe there were also bedbugs. She would have to wash everything from top to bottom, take inventory of the provisions, put patches on Barbe Zef's stuff, clear out the sheepfold of its piled-up filth. . . .

'Will I have enough time? Will I have time to do everything? . . . ' Mariutine asked herself almost in anguish. And suddenly her anxiety of not managing to finish what she had to do, and the difficulty of her tasks, too hard for her mere fourteen years, turned her thoughts elsewhere and she recalled the harsh and sharp exigencies of reality.

Even among the wretched hovels of the mountain folk, their own cabin was among the most wretched and bare and could not possibly have resembled the beautiful houses of the plain that she had seen—solid and well lit, with ample windows letting in the sun, and vast court-yards, barns, and stables. A bit of straightening up and cleaning would, nevertheless, make it less wretched and unsightly. If there were no provisions in the house—and usually when they returned they didn't find anything—it would also be necessary to induce Barbe Zef to give her money to buy whatever they needed.

Before, it was her mother who, with money received from the sale of the woodenwares, used to take care of provisions that allowed them to face the long winter with-out too much hardship. Now, it was Barbe Zef who had collected the money before leaving the hospice—a large sum, almost three hundred lire! Mariutine knew it, and tomorrow she meant to speak to him about it.

At this thought she was overcome with great shyness. She had never dealt with such things. She did not under-stand her uncle very well, but she knew that men do not willingly part with money. Again inexperience appeared like a fault to the fourteen-year-old, an element of failure.

'How much should I ask from him?' she wondered uneasily. 'We need flour, lard, oil, salt . . . If I ask too much, he'll lose his temper. Fifty lire? He'll give it to me . . . But for supplies for the whole winter maybe that's not enough.'

'A couple of wheels of cheese can be made out of the sheeps' milk,' she thought. 'The hen will lay some eggs that I'll keep for Rosùte. . . . Maybe forty lire for the rest is enough. Forty lire. Yes, yes, tomorrow I'll speak with him about it. Tomorrow I'll ask him for forty lire,' she repeated decisively. The difficulties and the work she was accustomed to, but the full weight and responsibility of which she felt for the first time upon herself alone, rather than alarming her suddenly made her calm.

She was needed now around the house. It was she who had to think about everything, figure things out, provide. She herself had to earn, she now had to earn food for herself and for Rosùte. *To earn it*. She did not want to be kept out of charity. She would earn it—provided that Barbe Zef would not force her to leave, not send her as a servant girl somewhere in the outside world, not separate her from Rosùte. . . .

It was only a few hours before dawn. There was no time to cry. Mariutine swiftly dried her tears. She stretched out on the bed next to her sister, and with a deep sigh she fell asleep.

✳

It is rare for the mountains to offer an image of serenity. More often they present a vision of violence and anguish, like a petrified torment, the drama of forms. The silence has the grandiose and unhuman quality of the solitude from which it derives. The solitude is so austere and motionless that it frightens the soul that questions it much more than does the ever-moving immensity of the ocean. Only when snow covers the mountains with its deathly softness do they apparently relent and grow soft in an illusion of peace. Even more rare are the days, under sunshine or under snow, on which the mountains truly *smile*.

That day was one of those: a clear day in October, cold, with a sky so polished and so still that it seemed made of crystal. The pastures were an intense green, and the peaks of Tudaio and Cridola gleamed in the sunshine as though strewn with a powder of silver. A trickle of water came from a boulder extremely high up, then vanished behind a hump, to reappear on the other side and shine for a moment among the beech trees.

When Mariutine awoke, Barbe Zef had already gone out into the woods. It had to be late, for the sun was high.

From the sheepfold insistent bleatings reached her ears. The bleating sheep were massed together against the door almost as if to call someone who might remember that it was time to open it. Mariutine, in her short underskirt and with her braids over her shoulders, opened the door wide and stood aside. The sheep, crowding and shoving against each other, went out.

There were seven, and while they were all about the same, she could tell one from the other. Often she amused herself by petting their wooly backs or taking the muzzle of one of them between her palms, searching out vainly the responsive look in their fixed depthless glassy pupils. Perhaps they too recognized Mariutine, because they obeyed her voice and her command. Without her help Petòti rarely succeeded in making them go and stay where he wanted them. Yet they passed by right in front of her, indifferent, with lowered heads, happy only in being freed, hurrying along toward the nearby meadow with their bouncy awkward gait, hip-hopping as barefoot people do.

Mariutine, who was watching over them from inside, saw them a bit later halted stock-still with the immobility of stone, their muzzles buried into the grass. They had obviously been neglected lately. They were skinny, without meat on their flanks, the long wool of their buttocks matted with dried dung.

Mariutine put on her wooden clogs and entered the sheepfold. The low-ceilinged enclosure, poorly ventilated by a grated window, measured just a few square meters, and it was piled incredibly high with filth.

'Barbe Zef must never have come to clean up in there,' Mariutine said to herself, sinking down to her knees in the dung. For two hours, with fork and spade, she shoveled, scraped, and carried manure outdoors, piling it a few meters from the hut but at a rather good distance from the stream, because the water was not to be contaminated. While working, she continually kept an ear tuned to hear if Rosùte were calling her. When she had finished, she plunged the pitchfork into the top of the heap like a banner and sat on the doorsill of the cabin breathing hard and fast.

Though nimble and healthy, she had finished a task beyond her powers, and she was flustered. Sweat fell in big drops along her cheeks, and her hair was getting into her eyes. Toiling with fork and spade had blistered the palms of her hands. Her arms, still a bit thin, childlike, and her sturdy legs of a mountain woman with muscled calves were covered with a kind of stinking, viscous, claylike plaster. Nevertheless, she contemplated her work with cheerful and satisfied eyes and felt infinitely more cheery, more tranquil and serene, than on previous days, or on those recent occasions when she had been toiling away in the hospice's vegetable garden and kitchens.

The cold fresh air whipped her face. Beneath the intensely blue sky even the poverty of the hut and the thankless work took on an appearance of happiness, of freedom, that subconsciously cheered her. She tucked up her skirt, ran to the stream, and immersed her legs up to where the delicate white skin was veined with blue. She felt the water, strong stinging and rapid, give her a kiss and a nip, and she experienced an impetuous joy.

✳

When she reentered the hut, she found Rosùte seated on the raised stone of the hearth, intent on sipping her milk. The little one had gotten washed and dressed all by herself. She had even tried to make the bed, and for all that effort she was less pale than usual, her face all smiles.

'Now I'm helping you,' she announced immediately at her sister's appearance. 'What can I do?'

'Nothing. You mustn't do anything. Let's see the foot.'

'But it's all better! Let me at least look after the sheep. My foot is all better!'

Mariutine followed the child with her eyes while she carefully came down from the step, putting down one little leg after the other, leaning against the doorpost. She went out across the meadow and reached the sheep which had scattered along the stream. Petòti, wagging his tail, ran to meet her.

Without wasting time, Mariutine got ready to inspect the cupboards to figure out what provisions were needed. As she had foreseen, there was nothing in the house, nothing except a little piece of rancid lard and those few half-rotted potatoes under the bed, among which, sorting and choosing, she managed to find seven or eight good ones. Buried in the straw mattress of their bed she discovered a half bottle of brandy, which she wrapped up in a rag and hid in the middle of her own belongings, hoping that Barbe Zef might have forgotten about it. What time was it? . . . Sun and shadow indicated almost eleven. Just time to light the fire and put the potatoes on to cook.

'Why was I so scared last night?' she wondered, cheerfully beating the lard on the cutting board. 'Rosùte feels better. Soon she'll be healed. Everything seemed complicated and difficult because I was tired! I was even scared to ask Barbe Zef for money for provisions, afraid that he would drive me out! But Barbe knows that we need provisions for the winter. He has almost three hundred lire. Why shouldn't he give me forty of them for the shopping? We won't be the only ones to eat; the greatest share he'll eat himself.'

Down deep, however, the thought of asking for money continued to worry her deeply, and, carrying lunch out to him in the woods towards midday, she decided to bring up the troubling topic with a long roundabout speech.

Barbe Zef did not show surprise nor did he raise the least difficulty. In fact, listening, he winked his eye and seemed satisfied. Yet the girl might not have been so trusting of this impression, if at the same time he had not drawn out four beautiful silver coins from a little sack kept between his shirt and skin. He looked at them, turned them around, and bounced them on the palm of his hand.

'Who's going to do the shopping?'

'I . . . ' murmured Mariutine timidly, fearing that he might want to go and might get drunk along the way.

'When?'

'As soon as possible. Before the snow closes the pass.'

Barbe Zef scratched his head.

'I would go,' he said, after having stood a moment in thought, 'but the wood I've been heaping is just about ready, and I can't leave it just now or all the charcoal might go bad.'

And without further ado he turned over to Mariutine the four silver coins.

Through that entire day and the following days, too, Barbe Zef remained in a good mood. And, strangely, he also chatted good naturedly and even ended up humming to himself in an undertone. He seemed a changed man. It seemed—though it grieved Mariutine to note it—that the *mâri*'s disappearance had relieved him of a heavy constraint, freed him from an incubus.

'Poor *mâri* . . .' thought Mariutine, 'she was so sick . . . If Barbe Zef would realize that, he wouldn't resent her peculiar ways and hold them against her.'

She had changed suddenly as at a single stroke. She had become closed in upon herself and cold even toward them, her own flesh and blood. She no longer kissed them. Asleep, she would curl up at the edge of the bed as far away and apart as possible, and she did not want to be touched. If baby Rosùte cuddled up against her in her sleep, she roughly pushed her away. And to justify Barbe Zef, Mariutine had to admit that in the last few years her mother's facial expression—and her glance and her obstinate silence—had been enough to cast coldness, like ice, and to stir something like antipathy—not only in those who knew her but also in strangers. Mariutine had seen it herself when they were traveling around to sell their stuff.

There exist privileged beings from whom, without their doing anything to bring it about, joy and serenity unconsciously emanate, beings who light up and bring gladness to the street through which they pass or the house into which they enter, who have in themselves something alive, friendly, and free. Others carry with them the heavy burden of bringing boredom or of upsetting anyone with whom they come in contact. If each person has a particular essence, a deep authenticity that determines a particular aura, the atmosphere Catine generated was one of sadness, discomfort, almost of frozen agony.

Ah, but it wasn't so for them. In dealing with her silence and the harshness of her few maternal words, they sensed her passionate love, her perpetual vigilance, and her jealous solicitude in which fear almost trembled. No, not for them! . . . But in others, poor *mâri*, in the others maybe yes. Without being at fault she produced this impression. Barbe Zef, too, who nevertheless was good.

The days and weeks passed, and life resumed its normal color, which is neither entirely bright nor entirely dark, but to girlish eyes most often tinted with a rosy hue. Work totally filled Mariutine's hours, and the grief in her heart abated. Her mother's image wasn't canceled out, no, but it was distanced, it paled, it became vague and less like reality.

Days of fair weather and sunshine continued, upon which followed sudden and rapid sunsets, and nights that were cold. Rosùte felt better and her cheeks filled out again red and firm. Twice Mariutine went down to the village to finish taking in supplies, for Barbe Zef had recognized the need to spend another forty lire so that they would have nothing to worry about for the whole winter.

Now that the coal making was done, he worked a plot of high ground rented from the commune, and Mariutine, having nimbly taken care of the housework, helped her uncle to rake the hay, gather it up in great bundles, and transport it to the grazing ground. She came down the mountain frequently during the day carrying loads that a donkey would have hardly been able to carry, and she never complained nor ever pleaded tiredness. She was the first to get up in the morning and the last to go to bed at night.

At home, without stinting on anything for anyone, she maintained an orderliness so strict and a way of economizing so tight and fast as to come close to avarice, fearing that they might not have enough provisions to last the whole winter. For Rosùte there were eggs and the best little tidbits and for Barbe Zef the biggest portions. For herself she grudged each morsel; her own part of the milk she set aside to make a few wheels of *çuc,* a kind of poor man's cheese, which she kept for herself and intended to sell.

Her ambition was to buy cloth for another set of sheets and that way to be able to change them at least once even in winter. For now, with only a single pair, they had to be both washed and dried in a single day, and in nasty or cold weather that was impossible. When she wasn't busy with the hay or the firewood, she would take the sheep to pasture, but never too far away because Rosùte must not get tired. She no longer went in the direction of the valley to search the horizon for a distant rising plume of smoke or to keep an ear tuned to whether the wind carried the sound of a human voice. Those were daydreams to which she no longer felt inclined.

She took the sheep into the beech woods or along the mountain stream relatively close to the hut. Afterwards she crossed through the stumps of Bosco Tagliato without any longer feeling either the childish fear of times past or the deep emotion she had felt the night of their return.

Calmness, returning to her heart, had given her back her trustful and happy nature. She had grown. She had become more graceful; her hair gleamed like a blaze of gold around her fresh face, and there was laughter in her eyes.

She would be fifteen in two months. For some time now she had taken to singing again. She taught Rosùte the old folk songs, and sometimes she made up new ones.

*

Not a soul had passed through those parts for a whole month; nor was that a novelty for Mariutine. The cheese factories of the high mountain had been emptied of people for quite a while, since all those who were not poor like them, at the first frosts, abandoned them in order to go lower down with their livestock. Now and then during the evening, when Barbe Zef and Rosùte were sleeping and she was lingering in the kitchen over her sewing, there flashed on her unexpectedly the sensation of total solitude, of silence so profound and empty that it tortured her. Then she lifted her eyes from her work and strained her ears to listen. Nothing . . . Not even the hooting of the owls. Not even the wind . . . Nothing.

Then Mariutine would bend her head over the faded skirt she was darning or over the huge patch that she was about to put on Barbe Zef's trousers. She didn't want to think about it. Didn't she know it? . . . Entire winters had passed sometimes when the *mâri* was still there without ever anyone knocking at the door—anyone at all. Only one time in so many years, an old man who had gotten lost at night instead of going down to the pass had turned up there by mistake. They had given him shelter in the hayloft until dawn. And another time a smuggler, like one possessed, with the customs officers at his heels: they had hidden him amid the sacks of charcoal.

But it was better that those strange visits should not happen.

Moreover, if the weather continued so fine, some acquaintance perhaps would be able to come. Winter seemed still far off. . . . One day or another, someone would come to call Barbe Zef for a pigsticking and sausage making, or for a sick animal. . . . Or even maybe . . . Pieri? . . .

Mariutine remembered having been brusque with him during their memorable journey, and she remembered also that he instead had been very good and patient with Rosùte. Pieri had said that before going overseas he might come. . . . Who could tell? But surely he had said that for no special purpose. Surely he wouldn't come for her after she had treated him so badly.

Who could tell? . . .

But the days were passing and Pieri did not come. Already the sky was no longer so clear, and towards sunset grey clouds came down from all directions, moving slowly, to cover the mountaintops and fill the valleys. The horizon that for only a few days before had stretched out boundless and clear to the sea sometimes contracted to just the tight gorge where the Zef cabin stood, hemmed in by a rock wall and a thicket of beech trees beyond which the eye could not see.

Night fell precipitately after a scant few hours of light. The stream had a hoarse and angry little voice that seemed spitefully to call forth the heavy autumn rains.

Pieri must already be in America, happy and satisfied in his cousin's shop, and who knew if he ever would return to Italy, and, if he did, whether he would return to these parts. Those who do not move from the mountains and do not know any other kind of life are satisfied with what they have and remain there, but those who have seen the world and have lived elsewhere find it difficult to come back. If Pieri made his fortune there in America, he would not remember the grazing ground where he was born, or, worse, he would think with horror about the wretched life in the mountains.

Days passed. Winter drew near. Winter, snow . . .

The memory of the cheerful and kind-hearted youth too faded away little by little. As the image of the dead gradually fades and recedes, so did the image of the absent youth fade and recede: his bold, sincere eyes; his blond curls; his hand that waved a last greeting; and after having thought about him almost every evening for many evenings, at last Mariutine did not think about him any more.

And then one grey and windy day, when the low skies foretold rain or snow, there he was! He appeared unexpectedly in front of them, at the head of the path descending to the mountain stream, like one who has been resurrected. He was wearing his good holiday suit, his hard new shoes, the broad, colored kerchief, and a nut-colored hat that he held tightly between his hands with a certain awkwardness.

'*Mandi, fantatis!* Good morning, girls!' he called from a distance, his voice and his bold sincere eyes spreading happiness all around.

Rosùte, who was minding the sheep along the stream while her sister was washing the clothes, ran to meet him, and hugged his knees, astonished and ecstatic.

'Pieri has come! Pieri has come!' she cried over and over.

And Petòti ran races of celebration back and forth at top speed barking as though he had gone crazy.

Mariutine almost let the clothes she had been soaping slip into the water.

Pieri had come!

And he sits down upon a stone near them, for safety's sake putting his fine hat on the grass. And they don't know what else to say.

Luckily Rosùte keeps the conversation going. Tugging

69

at his hair, she comes out with a string of questions: if he is no longer going to sea, and when is he going, and how long it took him to walk the road from his place to where they were, and how come not finding them at home he had guessed that they were at the stream.

'I'm a wizard,' the youth replies. 'All I have to do is close my eyes, and I know all I want to know.'

'Can you do magic too?'

'Sure! If you want I'll do a magic trick for you too. Come here.'

But Rosùte doesn't want him to do magic for her and she runs far away laughing. He has tied a red rag to Petòti's tail. Petòti has gone completely out of control and runs this way and that, scaring the sheep.

There is one great big sheep among them there with a black muzzle and a sly manner, who takes advantage of the hubbub to go off on her own. All the other sheep behind her leap up from mound to mound; they scatter. Rosùte, flanked by Petòti, must run after them and lead them back.

'Careful for your foot!' Mariutine cries to her.

'I don't even recall that it hurt!' the little girl triumphantly announces from above.

'Is it true that it's healed?' asks Pieri.

'Not so well as she says. If she's tired, it still swells up, and her little leg too.'

Mariutine beats her laundry vigorously in the thin stream of water that runs skipping down among the stones. Pieri whistles nonchalantly.

Finally she says to him, indifferently, without looking at him, 'I thought that you'd left.'

And he: 'I said I would come and I've come.'

Then they keep quiet again.

'Mariùte,' he says all at once, all in one breath, and it is obvious that he had come on purpose to tell her this, 'I was wrong that night when we climbed up the mountain together. I laughed and chatted without considering that you were heartsick, that you had just lost your *mâri*. But I swear that it wasn't meanness. First I had forgotten, and later I didn't know how to make up for that. But I've thought about it so much, since then, and I came up for this very reason: to ask your pardon, to apologize and offer condolences, and to make up with you, if you think I'm worthy of that.'

The somewhat solemn and evidently prepared speech had such a sincere basis of decency and good will, that Mariutine was moved.

'I've never been angry with you, Pieri,' she whispered, lifting her lovely blue eyes to him for the first time. 'It is I who should ask your pardon, for having been so rude, that evening. . . . But I was very tired, and then . . . you can imagine. . . . When are you leaving? Are you actually going away? You haven't changed your mind?'

'No,' said Pieri, 'I'm sorry about going away for my *mâri's* sake, and for a good many other reasons as well, but I haven't changed my mind. I'm going away so that I can come back one day and not need to stay up here any longer. I don't know if you understand what I mean. If I decided not to leave, if I were to give up on trying my luck now while I'm young and have someone to help me where I'm going, I would have to stay on the mountain for the rest of my life. It's a fine outlook for those who like it, but not for me. To me it would seem like being tied to a chain like a brute animal. To have a crust of bread, here, one has to eke out a miserable living all year, to do without, and struggle with the woods, the snow, the mountain, the summer that comes too late and the winter that comes too soon: struggle from morning until night, suffer, and all without help, without comfort or convenience, alone like a dog, because grazing grounds are remote from each other and the towns are still further yet; whole months go by, you know it, when roads are not passable and you go without seeing a soul. That's why I want to try my luck. If God helps me, within four years, I hope to return with enough money to buy a small house and a field. Oh, I'm not talking about in the plain, which I don't care for, nor about remaining idle when I come back, for that would please me even less, but I'd like to be a bit more lower down from the clouds than where we are now, and I'd like to work a bit more like a human being. Four years. Now I'm nineteen. At twenty-three, I'll be able to return.'

Pieri had spoken with earnestness and conviction, like a man, and it was clear that what he was saying must have been thought over and rethought at great length. He waited a bit so that Mariutine might express judgment or approval, but Mariutine kept quiet, and so he resumed whistling in order to save face.

'You, how old are you?' he asked abruptly.

'Fifteen, . . . ' replied the girl, flaming up in blushes. 'I'm going on fifteen.'

And they said no more. Rosùte had gathered the sheep, and Pieri was in a hurry to get started on his trip home before nightfall.

Mariùte collected her wet clothes. 'There's little water,' she said. 'I can hardly do the wash with so little water. Let's walk a little ways together.'

They all walked on. The sheep and Petòti formed the advance guard, and Rosùte, as on that night already long ago, took hold of Pieri's hand.

'How will you cross the sea? In a boat? A big boat? and what if a hurricane comes?' she asked, looking up to him and hanging on every word from his lips.

Then Pieri explained that his boat was called a ship, indeed a steamer, and that it was big . . . at least as big as the church of Calalzo or Pieve . . . and all made of iron— that is, of iron inside and wood on the outside, otherwise how could it stay afloat?—and with so many machines and mechanisms that, even if a hurricane came, there was nothing to fear.

'One is at sea from thirty to forty days, and there's no danger. Sometimes it does happen that a ship sinks,' he asserted with the sure competence of an experienced mariner, 'but almost never. And in any case, why should it happen just this time when I'm aboard? I'm lucky,' he proclaimed merrily.

In his words there was still a bit of the boyish bravado that, on the night of their return, had made him tell his exploits, exaggerating them quite a bit, but it was a boastfulness more apparent than real. It was mainly the trust and sense of security linked to the happy disposition of one who tends to view things in the best possible light and ignore anything sad.

'Is it true that there are sharks in the ocean?'

'Sure, and there are ever so many of them, hundreds and hundreds, and they follow the steamers with their mouths open wide like so many ovens. If you fall into the water, they gobble you up in one gulp.'

'Then don't fall,' Rosùte urged him seriously.

'Where do you get the boat?' asked Mariutine.

'In Genoa. Monday. Genoa's a lovely city. I'll send you a postcard. And then my address after I get to Argentina. But you . . . will you answer me?' he asked almost bashfully, and his bright eyes unselfconsciously searched Mariutine's.

'We don't know how to write!' proudly proclaimed Rosùte.

'Really? This is bad. You must learn.'

A strong wind had come up that chased the clouds this way and that through the sky, driving them forward like a flock towards the valleys. Through a broad rift could be seen the opposite mountain, which appeared violet, and the ridges all around appeared bruised and livid. The voice of the rushing stream reached them hoarser and more furious.

'There won't be snow, but it'll rain buckets,' said Pieri.

73

'If I get home before the deluge hits, I can call myself lucky.'

'But you said that you are like that, lucky!' exclaimed Rosùte. 'It won't rain! You'll stop the clouds.'

And they all began to laugh.

'How are you getting along? How does Barbe Zef treat you?' Pieri asked Mariutine in an undertone.

'Very well,' she replied. 'We really can't complain about anything.'

'Give him my regards,' said Pieri soberly.

The conversation languished, carried on exclusively by Rosùte. Thunder was beginning to rumble far off, with the dull and muffled din of an enormous cart rolling up and down through the skies. Nevertheless, instead of hurrying, Pieri slowed his steps, and so did Mariutine, who was always in a hurry. Now she walked like an ant.

'Pieri, do you know that I've learned to sing?' asked Rosùte. 'I know three songs. Mariutine taught them to me.'

'Only three?'

'But when you come back, I'll know a hundred of them, and maybe a thousand.'

'Pum!' laughed the youth. 'Too many! But it is surely a good thing to sing. . . . What bothers me is that over there I won't hear our own folk songs any more. For us from around here, that's like going without our daily bread. You, you sang very well, once . . . ' he added turning toward Mariutine.

'Mariùte!' Rosùte entreated, letting go of Pieri's hand to run and take her sister's. 'Let Pieri hear the last one you taught me, the one that's so nice!'

'But he already knows it, it's not new,' Mariutine tried to shrug her off.

'Which one?'

'Lùs la lune, criche l'albe' . . . 'The moon's on high, the dawn approaches.' Don't you know it?'

'A little.'

'Then let's all three of us sing it together. Yes, please, let's sing it!' pleaded Rosùte.

The moon's on high, the dawn approaches,
Now the farmer's up and around,
And all the birds about are singing,
How they set my heart to pound.

Fly through the woods and through the mountains,
Fly, oh larks, for my true love's sake,
Fly also through the countryside
And sing the secret of heartache.

My heart has been so badly pierced
But don't disclose by whom 'twas done,
Don't name the one who has hurt me so,
I hope he'll return, but don't name the one.

They had all three joined hands and were singing as they walked along, nodding their heads in accompaniment to the rhythm of the song. The child in the middle, happy, with her eyes fixed on her sister's lips, waited to take the pitch from her and to see approval or blame in her glance. Her fragile voice came forth with a fervor that made her eyes shine and her cheeks flame. She concentrated on how to imitate Mariutine even in the way of holding her head which, like her sister, she threw back a bit the better to free her voice. From time to time she cast a quick look at Pieri, as though to say to him: 'You hear how I sing?'

Fly through the woods and through the mountains,
Fly, oh larks, for my true love's sake,
Fly also through the countryside
And sing the secret of heartache.

There was something touching in the words and in the tune of this song, something melancholy and profound in the long and drawn-out last notes of every phrase. The young voices faded away into thin air without raising an echo, yet the unsmiling skies and all of nature surrounding them—arid hostile and relentless—seemed full of their own good feeling.

Mariutine did not dare look at her companion, but, in the way women know, even so, *she saw him*. She noticed his lovely eyes, his curly hair. She heard his voice warm and melodious blending with her own without hesitation, following hers, harmonizing with and supporting hers instinctively.

They were both blond, the girl of an enkindled blondness, the youth paler and almost faded. Both had fair skin, intensely blue eyes, and fine features, as people of Carnia often have when young. Pieri was taller than Mariutine, nimble and sturdy. He wore good clothes, with a tie and a new, a brand-new hat.

Mariutine was almost intimidated by the elegance of his getup, and for the first time she experienced a confused sense of uneasiness about her short and faded skirt, all patches and darns, and about the rags he had seen her washing, which she was now carrying on her arm, so threadbare that they showed the weave of the cloth. But this confused sensation of shame for her great poverty, and an instinctive womanly preoccupation with her appearance, were overpowered by a great sweetness, a feeling of joy and excitement never before experienced. This feeling was so strong and deep that it almost turned into melancholy.

The three had begun to sing timidly in subdued voices. Then they had gone along gathering courage. The final stanza was repeated twice full throated.

My heart has been so badly pierced
But don't disclose by whom 'twas done,
Don't name the one who has hurt me so,
I hope he'll return, but don't name the one.

By now they had reached the spot where they would have to part. The wind was blowing strongly, scattering the clouds that were being torn asunder here and there and revealing gaps of sky. Beneath the strange light the meager pastures, sparse with low shrubs and rocky out-croppings, seemed yellow. The sheep standing close against each other blended with the boulders, their color that of grass scorched by the wind.

Although some raindrops had begun to fall, Pieri drew a knife out of his pocket and stayed a few moments more to carve a little wand for Rosùte. 'I'm leaving you this to remember me by,' he said. 'I'll come back to reclaim it in four years.' The words were addressed to Rosùte, but his eyes rested candidly and soberly on Mariutine.

As on the last occasion, goodbyes were rapid. Pieri kissed Rosùte on both cheeks and gave his hand to Mar-iutine, a bit pale, with the stiff arm and awkward gesture of country people. Then he went off almost running and without turning to look back, as on that other night long before. At the bend he waved his kerchief high. The crunching and bouncing of pebbles could be heard under his feet as he descended, and then all was again solitude and silence.

*

That night the wind continued to whistle without inter-ruption, and at a certain hour it blew more violently than ever. The cabin shuddered from its foundations to the roof, seeming to sway back and forth on its base. The wooden walls creaked as though they would crash down from one moment to the next, and the broad stones set on the rooftop to keep it in place flew off this way and that like twigs.

The storm lasted several hours, and then the wind abruptly subsided. And the pelting rain began. More than a simple rainfall, it was a cloudburst. It was as though after the long drought the heavens had opened their cataracts wide to pour down upon the mountain.

In Barbe Zef's storeroom and in the sheepfold, which were exposed to the north wind, water penetrated forcefully through the old dilapidated roof, flooding the ground and flowing along as though it were a stream. The sheep bleated complainingly, the hens fluttered around as though blind knocking their stupid heads against the wall. Barbe Zef had to shelter the livestock in the kitchen, where at least, although there too the water was coming down in a dark rivulet along the chimney, one nearly dry corner could still be found.

For the next eight days, night and day, the rain fell without pause, widening and worsening the breach on the roof. They had to resign themselves to granting the sheep and the hens permanent residence in the kitchen. Barbe Zef too, after having resisted for two nights, the third evening took his straw mattress and his sopping, mud-splattered covers in one armful and found them a better place on top of Catine's wedding chest.

This business took place without a word said and so matter of factly that Mariutine did not even dare to show she had noticed it. If she had not had in mind her mother's prohibition, she herself would have suggested before the end of the first night that poor Barbe Zef move his stuff into their wretched little room.

Of course there was little space for a third person, but they had to recognize that the poor man was not the least nuisance. He lay down to sleep after they did and he was the first to get up. Toward dawn he would cough and spit a bit—that was natural: someone else would have caught pneumonia from having wallowed in the water that way! but for the remainder of the night he slept in a leaden slumber.

His continuous and deep snoring, like the death's rattle of a huge beast, at first rather disturbed the girls, especially Rosùte, who was easily upset and could hardly fall asleep, and when she did would wake with a terrified start, huddling close to her sister: 'What's that?' . . . But then they both ended by getting used to it.

Mariutine, too, no longer found it so strange as at the beginning to catch a glimpse of that great balding head just a few steps away from them, tousled with scant reddish hair, and that outline of a man's body stretched out motionless under the dark woolen blanket, looking like a corpse on top of a coffin. And as they had gotten used to the roar of the torrent, the uninterrupted raging of the rainfall, and the promiscuity of the sheep and the hens—as one gets used to everything in this world—the girls at last also got accustomed to Barbe Zef's nightly presence. Finally they didn't pay attention to him any more.

At last the rain stopped. In one single night the sky became utterly clear again, the surrounding mountains splendidly distinct. The air took on a marvelous purity and transparence.

Since it was impossible to repair the roof quickly, as it was soaked through and rotting and already completely collapsing, that project was put off until springtime. Instead Barbe Zef took advantage of the good weather to return to the woods to finish gathering the great store of firewood, anticipating that a snowfall would allow him to load it on his sled and fetch it home. Mariutine helped him willingly, knowing well that winter now would come all at once like a betrayal, and that life would then be confined within the cabin's four walls.

She began anew carrying loads of firewood from the forest to the little shed adjoining the cabin that the bad weather had miraculously spared. All over again she reviewed the state of their provisions. She counted the eggs, the little shapes of cheese in a row on the board. With a strict eye she considered the flour, the oil, the lard that had to last until spring. Rosùte too took part in preparing for the extreme cold. She ran here and there through the house with some rag in her hand searching for holes and cracks to stuff.

79

The glittering sun shone in the intensely blue sky, and yet winter was present, like an expected guest who barefoot, quick, and silent, was on the way and would abruptly throw open the door and say: 'I'm here.'

In fact, after days that were beautiful and almost mild, the wind resumed its whistling. It was no longer the inconstant, teasing wind content to frolic with the bushes and the low grass, nor its impetuous and wrenching brother that had uncovered the roof of the sheepfold, passing stiff winds after which quickly followed the calm. It was a grandiose wind that came from afar with broad blasts and a solemn and profound rhythm. And it carried the scent of snow, the frozen breath of glaciers. It violently throttled the summits of the high woods, howled at length through the gorges, and descended to the valley with the roaring of the mountain torrent. It spread out its fatal announcement not only over the mountain, but over all of nature.

Its harsh and majestic music lasted three days. Then one morning when Mariutine awoke, she was surprised by a strange silence. The woods, the steep hills, and the valleys were covered with snow, and more snow, more snow, and more snow. More snow was falling silent deep and tranquil.

*

Winter had begun.

In the Zef cabin the hours soon assumed their winter rhythm. Through the glass of the little window light reached in from the diffuse whiteness of the mountains rather than from the sky. An intense cold enveloped the sleeping earth like a shroud. At four o'clock it was already necessary to light a lamp, and all of life revolved around the fire, constantly lit, red and crackling in the low fireplace. Chores quickly dispensed with, Mariutine used the hours to knit socks or mend some old garment. With a knife Barbe Zef carved a piece of soft wood and worked from it bizarre figures, toys, kitchen utensils. Rosùte played with Petòti, or lifted herself up onto a chair and, with her nose flattened against the panes of the tiny window, watched the snow descend, descend interminably.

In the low-ceilinged, small kitchen the sheep and the hens caused an unbearable stink, but no one seemed to notice. Barbe Zef passed whole days without opening his mouth, and if he ever did speak, it was about how deep the snow was, how much had fallen during the night, or to venture a prediction about its duration and the condition of the roads. Mariutine and Rosùte listened with a keen and almost anxious interest, quite different from that of children who live in more densely populated centers, for whom living conditions, well-being, and life itself are not so contingent upon phenomena of nature.

One day Barbe Zef prepared the sled and went out to move some wood. He returned with his hair and moustache flecked with small white flakes that melted rapidly in the fire's heat. He shook himself and shrugged like a soaked dog, then squatted with his back to the fire to get dry. He winked his eye and seemed to be laughing, but Mariutine, who knew him well, understood at once that he was in a bad mood.

'If the snow goes any higher, no one will want to call me for the pig or the cows,' he mumbled after a long silence. 'And I will not even be able to sell the coal. This year, this is how every chance to earn money will be lost.'

Next day Mariutine lit the lamp an hour later than usual and put only a wee, almost invisible piece of lard into the soup.

Changeless days passed one after another. Evenings and nights were long and frozen.

It was carnival time! . . . In the evening, when Barbe Zef and her sister had gone to bed and she stayed alone to sew beside the fire, without wanting to Mariutine would think that at that time and hour, in certain cabins lower down, people were having parties, playing cards, and eating roasted chestnuts. Someone was playing the accordion. Boys and old men sang along in chorus, and some folks danced. . . . Yes, even for the poor, winter was not the same all over. On a scale of privations and sacrifice there was still a bit of difference, fate still played favorites.

But she was not considering those things with envy or rancor. Rather it was as she might have thought about unrealizable and marvelous dreams: as she might have thought about a fairy tale. Who in the world would have been able to come to their place? Where would they ever have been able to have a party like that? . . . To have a party one had to have a good warm barn, with several cows, and oil for the lamp, a small 'collation,' at least eight or ten chairs, a bench, a pack of cards. . . . Dreams.

Another thought, which seemed closer to reality, occupied her attention and kept her company. Pieri. . . . Four years. . . . Maybe Pieri might return in four years.

For people from the country or from the mountains, inured to long patience, four years of waiting are not so terrible. Engagements sometimes last even ten years, and it happens that one who departed with blond or brown hair returns with grey locks to claim the girl with whom he had exchanged vows before going away. Sometimes he finds her dried out and mouldering and he takes her for his wife all the same. Sometimes he does not return at all or he returns with another bride—but that is rare.

Between Pieri and her there had been no engagement. . . . Just something, something in the air, in the silences, in their eyes. Some nameless thing that made her heart beat faster. . . . But Pieri was not for her; or better *she* was not the fiancée who could be worthy of Pieri upon his return, if he returned. Maybe if he had been poor, maybe. . . . But Pieri, who found mountain life hard and had left to improve his lot, did not know—did not even remotely know—what poverty was.

His family was one of the more well to do and highly regarded of those who among the herd keepers constituted a type of aristocracy. These were people of old lineage, well provided with everything, proud and eager to look after their property. His brothers had married well, finding wealthy brides among the women of Calalzo and Lorenzago. As for his mother, Mariutine had seen her a few times. . . . She was a petite woman who, when she went down to the village for the big celebrations, put on a silk apron, with gold jewelery around her neck. She was one of the few who still wore the traditional costume. But when she met Mariutine, even though she knew her, she did not condescend to look at her.

No, though she was still almost a child, Mariutine understood, and nurtured no illusions. Pieri was not for her. Even if he were to return in four years, he would look for some woman of a station comparable to his own, not a barefoot orphan who takes the sheep to pasture or goes traveling through the countryside to sell colanders and serving spoons. What a disgrace that would be for his proud family! And then the mother. . . .

How Pieri resembled her! . . . He had her blue eyes and refined features, but with an expression of kindness and courtesy she did not have. Pieri was friendly and cheerful and not at all stuck-up. It was enough to see him smile to understand how good he was. Then he had a candid way of looking someone in the eyes while saying things that inspired trust and friendship. And those handsome blond curls. . . .

He had said he would send a postcard from Genoa and his address. . . . Would he remember? . . . In any case she wouldn't be able to reply. She did know how to read a bit, but as for writing, she could barely write her name.

'Able neither to write nor to sew, at age fifteen!' the nuns had commented in a tone of severe reproof.

But how should she have learned to write, far as they

83

were from schools? How should she have learned to sew, if all the years of her lifetime she had had to labor at strenuous, primitive, toilsome tasks generally done by a man or an animal? . . . And in truth it almost pleased her more to work hard outdoors than to remain sitting on a chair patching clothes. Now she did it out of necessity, but she would by far have preferred cutting firewood in the forest, or carrying huge bundles of hay on her shoulders, or at least taking the flock to pasture.

Sometimes a restless impatience seized her over those days that were always the same, over the heavy and fetid air of the little kitchen, and over that shut door and that tiny window opaque as a wall. There came over her an impulse to run outside in the wind and the rain and the snow. That motionless silence choked her. She felt she would have gone down to the plain and climbed back up the mountain again all in one breath, if someone had said to her: 'Go.'

At such times, four years seemed to her long, interminable, an eternity. She had found a piece of broken mirror, not even as wide at the palm of a hand, and when she was quite certain that no one would see her, she looked at herself fleetingly. She was almost surprised by that hair of hers so blond, those eyes so blue. She smiled, perplexed at her image, stroking her braids with her hand. . . . But what, after all, were they, those four years? Four winters, four springs, four brief summers. . . . A flash of lightning.

'I said I would come and I came.'

She would be almost nineteen, then. . . .

'I said I would come and I came.'

Four years, an eternity. Four years, a lightning flash.

＊

And one morning while she was busy about the house putting their poor belongings in order, without knowing how or why—maybe not even thinking about Pieri, maybe simply because youth has a need to live—

Mariutine began to sing full-throatedly, with an abandon-
ment and joy she hadn't experienced for a long while:

My heart has been so badly pierced
But don't disclose by whom 'twas done,
Don't name the one who has hurt me so,
I hope he'll return, but don't name the one.

For some days now Barbe Zef had had a change of
mood. It was hardly daybreak when he would go out with
his shovel to work around the cabin, or to reopen the
narrow path hemmed in like a trench between two high
walls that the snow built up higher every night. Or else he
went to the stable contriving to separate the rotted boards
from the good ones for the next repairs. But when he
would return towards noon, all soaked and numb, he
would throw his shovel into a corner and sit down to sulk
morosely by the fire, irritated and mumbling to himself.

Being cooped up by the terrible weather had lasted for
a month now, first the rain and then the snow. It obviously got on his nerves. And maybe something else also
bothered him deeply. He was accustomed, even in winter,
when all hell didn't break loose as it had this year, to go
down at least twice a week and roam around the houses
and pubs, selling his coal and making small talk with this
one and that one of his acquaintances. This year, on the
other hand, he had had to stay put, always in the same
place.

Rosùte wasn't aware of anything, but Mariutine had
noticed the change and was worried. Not only because of
Barbe Zef's bad mood, but also because, when he thought
nobody watched, he would ramble through the house,
rummaging in the drawers and peering under the credenza like one who is searching for something and doesn't
want to be noticed.

One day, unexpectedly coming into the little sleeping
room, the girl caught him rummaging in the straw mat-

tress of their bed. At her appearance he drew back grumbling.

'He's searching for the bottle,' thought Mariutine, and her heart sank.

That evening, while she was stirring the polenta, two or three times she felt Barbe Zef's eyes fixed on her with a furtive look, full of rancor. She turned, and at once those eyes were avoiding her. With the steaming polenta turned upside down on the cutting board, she placed before him his portion of the soup with the biggest chunk of lard in it. He began to eat greedily, his head close to the soup bowl. From his usual somewhat obtuse face there could not be guessed one single thought, neither kind nor evil.

＊

Those impressions too vanished rapidly. The sky hinted at brightening. Through the narrow vale there passed slight gusts of wind churning the snow into powder and making it eddy almost dry through the air. There was a saying among the mountain people that that was the sign of imminent clearing.

And a worry more serious than the one roused by Barbe Zef's bad mood left Mariutine anxious. Rosùte's foot, perhaps because she hadn't been exercising it, perhaps because of the season's dampness, had swelled up all over again, and the swelling, hard and inflamed and of abnormal color, was rising up through the leg almost toward the knee. The child dragged herself around through the cabin for several days limping, and she must have had a fever. One morning she could no longer get out of bed. Lying flat, she did not suffer so much, but if she put her foot on the ground, she howled with pain.

When Barbe Zef found out how things stood, he neither became sullen nor did he show worry. Without saying a word, he went out with his nails and hammer to repair the breach in the roof, for, thank God, the weather had finally turned fair again. Between one hammer blow and the next, Mariutine heard him whistle cheerfully. When he came back to eat, even before he downed his first mouthful, he said, 'It's time to settle this business with the foot. Thursday the doctor in Forni holds his clinic. I'll take the *frute* to pay him a visit.'

Thursday. Just one day away. It was a long day of despair for Rosùte, who absolutely did not want to hear anything about the visit and the doctor, and a day of great indecision for Mariutine. It seemed to her a very dangerous moment to risk crossing the valley; on the other hand, to oppose the visit would have been a real mistake, for Rosùte's ailment had dragged on far too long. But was it possible to let her go alone with Barbe Zef, as frightened and suffering as she was?

Barbe Zef had assured her that on the journey he would always be carrying Rosùte in his arms, and on this she could rely, but who would have said an affectionate word to her, if she was in pain? . . . Barbe Zef had not been made for those things. As for all three of them going down together to Forni, to that he would have objected. Mariutine was sure of it, whether out of concern for the flock or for leaving the hut unoccupied. Never mind! . . . Whatever Barbe Zef would say . . .

The next morning Mariutine leapt out of bed before dawn. Her heart was pounding hard. She paused a second behind the kitchen door without daring to open it, then with quick resolution threw it wide open. *He* was there, and he was greasing his shoes with meat fat.

'Barbe Zef, now I'll dress Rosùte, and I'm coming with you to take her to the doctor's.'

And Barbe Zef, without raising his head, rather than getting angry or discussing the matter, replied calmly, 'Don't take too long about it, for it's late.'

Rosùte, when she heard that her sister would be going with her, at once relaxed and let herself be persuaded. Getting her dressed was a serious affair, involving as it did

87

making her a bandage, for during the night the knee had become as big as a baby's head, and, as Mariutine had foreseen, it would be an even more serious affair to go adventuring through the mountains.

The day was clear and without wind, but the snow fallen on the preceding days was so deep and still so fresh and soft that at every step one sank into it. Moreover, as always happens, the mountain beneath the snow had lost its distinctive contours and no longer offered any point of reference. Just outside the little vale where the Zefs lived, which formed a kind of corridor, it looked like an immense basin white smooth and soft, crowned by the very highest peaks. Doubly treacherous in its apparent smoothness, neither its heights nor its depths could any longer be perceived. Every trace of mule track had disappeared. Only some snow-laden trees emerged here and there lost in the midst of an immense whiteness—and even these were buried to halfway up the trunk.

But by now the decision had been made, and the three set out on their way. For a long time they were followed by the desperate yelps of Petòti, who had been locked up in the kitchen. Then all was merciless silence.

On the improvised stretcher, under a thick wool cover, Rosùte lay on her back, with her rigidly extended little leg looking enormous, and Barbe Zef and Mariutine, shod in broad snowshoes, did their best to carry her gently and without jolts, but the soft snow rendered their task so arduous that at every step of the way the little girl uttered a moan. Covering up her uneasiness, Mariutine sought to distract her and keep her cheerful, and in the meantime not to lose sight of Barbe Zef's movements, though she was terrified that he would miss the road. There was danger, in case the correct way was lost, of foundering and falling into the ravines.

But Barbe Zef had good strong legs and a sure instinct. He never strayed from the mule track, and if he did swerve, he immediately took it up again. The crossing of the valley lasted four hours. As God willed it, the three arrived at Forni.

*

In the waiting room of the outpatient clinic there were quite a few people. Almost all of them were women with babes in their arms, come from far away. An old man, who seemed to be holding onto his soul with his teeth, jaundiced even in his eyes, supported under the armpits by his son, likewise had come on foot, and he had been on the road for over an hour. While they were waiting their turn, the women chatted amongst themselves, telling each other about their children's illnesses with great fullness of detail. A child here and there, bored with waiting, was whimpering.

There was one child, not an infant, three or four years old, in his mother's arms, with an enormous swollen head and two thin, limp legs which dangled down inertly. From time to time he would emit a sort of complaining moan, and then the mother got up from the bench where she had been sitting and paced up and down through the room lulling him and clapping him with little pats on his back. A pregnant woman, with a flower-patterned kerchief on her head, stood near the window sucking at an orange.

Every so often the door leading to the doctor's examining room would open to let someone enter, and at every such entering those still waiting stared at the door, which closed again smoothly and gently. Then the subdued chatting of the women resumed, as did the whinings of the children.

When it was Rosùte's turn, the examination was very brief. The doctor, a gruff man in his fifties clad in a long white coat, as soon as he uncovered the leg, declared that it definitely was a serious matter and there was no question of taking the child home. They would have to leave her in the hospital where appropriate equipment for treatment was available.

'Aren't you from below Forni?' he asked Barbe Zef.

'Yessir.'

'Then it's all right.'

The assistant wrote a few lines on a form and delivered it to the nurse. The stretcher arrived and Rosùte disappeared howling down a long corridor.

'Doctor, sir . . . ' ventured Mariutine, all agitated and shaky, 'wouldn't it be possible to . . . '

'What? Do you want your sister cured? Then there's nothing to do but leave her here. You can come to see her once a week. But it's better if you don't come to see her. Sick people heal more quickly when they're removed from members of their own household.'

And that was all. It had all happened so fast that Mariutine and Barbe Zef found themselves outside the door of the hospital, in the middle of the deserted street, without even knowing how. Mariutine felt more perturbed and unhappy than she had ever felt before, even when her mother died. Rosùte without her, Rosùte in the hospital, the equipment and machines there. . . . Above all what tormented her was her young sister's despair. She imagined, she *heard* her sister's howls, remembering vividly the scenes that Rosùte had made when sent from the hospice with a little lie, sent away without Mariutine to the villa of Donna Emmelina.

She sat down on a wayside stone and began to cry. Barbe Zef stood for a bit looking at her without knowing what to say. Evidently the tragedy did not seem so serious to him; as a matter of fact he took it with a great deal of philosophy.

'I'm going over here for a moment; I'll be back,' he said winking his eye, and he hastily departed.

One of the women who had brought her baby to the doctor, and who was the last to leave with a prescription in her hand, noticed the crying girl, and went up to her.

'You should never cry,' she said. 'It's not at all so bad in the hospital. The doctor makes you feel a bit embarrassed at the beginning, but he's kind. I spent three months under his care and I got cured.'

'But she's very small, a little girl who was used to staying all the time with me . . . ' sobbed Mariutine.

Bells were striking noon; the small shops along the street were closing. A band of schoolchildren passed at a run with their book satchels strapped to their shoulders like knapsacks. Some workingmen on their bicycles went by, and then a cripple in a sort of low carriage drawn by a dog. The good woman with her baby in her arms, too, having exchanged a few more words with Mariutine, said goodbye and left.

'I have five more kids at home,' she said, stroking the head of the baby she held in her arms. 'This is the littlest. He has that whooping cough: when he gets an attack, I'm afraid he's going to die. *Mandi!* And be brave!'

The midday bustle had lasted just a few minutes, and the street had become deserted once more.

Mariutine was still seated on the wayside stone, all by herself.

⁎

The hospital's façade extended in front of her white and regular, its large windows curtainless. Mariutine anxiously ran her gaze over all those windows one by one, with the naive hope of seeing—who knows?—her dear Rosùte, or at least of hearing her voice. But no one appeared, and full though it was of people, not one voice came from the building, as if it were completely uninhabited. Only from time to time, at regular intervals, from an isolated pavilion at the distant end of the lawn surrounding the hospital on three sides, a howl tore the silence, and fell into the silence. The crazy ones must be staying back there.

The wing of a nun's white headdress passed rapidly

behind the panes of a big window. The tinkling of a bell could be heard. Then nothing more.

Mariutine remembered all at once that Barbe Zef had said that he would be coming right back, and he had been gone for almost an hour. Yes, when they had come out of the hospital it was half past eleven, and now look, it was past noon. Barbe Zef was not to be seen.

The girl dried her eyes, got up, and began to walk back and forth with small steps in front of the hospital door. To go away would be worse. Barbe Zef would come and not find her. And then, where was she to go?

The town consisted of this single street, flanked by irregular modest little houses interrupted by vegetable gardens. Then it broadened into a small open square. At the far end of the street Mariutine saw protruding halfway up the façade of a house lower than the others a wrought iron decoration in whose center the painted figure of a white horse stood out. This ornament swayed lightly in the wind. She drew near and read the inscription: *Inn and stable at the Little White Horse.*

The door and windows of the inn had drawn red curtains, but the door was ajar, and from the opening could be seen a long and narrow entrance hall, with some tables of silver fir, and at the rear the proprietor's desk, dark. At the *focolare,* which was behind the proprietor's desk, the fire blazed up merrily, and a young woman, seated on a stool with her back to the flames, was nursing an infant.

Mariutine stopped, undecided, to peer through the opening of the doorway. The inn was almost deserted. Only an elderly workman, at a table near the entrance, was nibbling bread and salami, and at one of the tables at the rear was Barbe Zef with two other men. In front of them they had a bottle and three glasses, and they were talking together.

Not daring to enter, she just stood there and stared,

hoping that Barbe Zef might turn toward her, or that from one instant to the next he would get up to leave, but Barbe Zef seemed to have put down roots in that inn, and to have completely forgotten her existence.

Powerful feelings, fatigue, and going without food had put a great chill over Mariutine. Her feet were soaked and her legs numbed up to the knees. Even though she held her mother's heavy shawl around her shoulders, she kept shivering. Meanwhile time passed. After waiting uselessly for a good while the girl lightly pushed aside the door's shutter and stuck her head in.

'Barbe Zef . . . ' she called quietly. Then more loudly, 'Barbe Zef!'

Barbe Zef turned abruptly, his glass in his hand, and he seemed annoyed. But he immediately regained his cheerfulness.

'What are you doing out there? Come in, come in, for gosh sakes,' he exclaimed. 'Before going back up, we'll need to have a bite. Ahi, host, a glass and a bowl of soup also for this *fantate*.'

Mariutine entered timidly and sat at the table with the three men. One of them, who seemed the most important, an elderly, corpulent individual, wore a short cape with a rabbit fur collar. He was dressed more like an artisan or a merchant than like a farmer. The other wore a gold ring in his left ear and had on his shoulders a full riding cape whose tails touched the ground. Barbe Zef poured Mariutine a glass of red wine. The host put in front of her a tin tablespoon and a bowl of steaming soup, rich and oily, steamingly aromatic. From the *focolare* a bit of heat reached her.

Forcing herself, she began to eat the soup in small spoonfuls. So strong was her worry about Rosùte that it made her hardly able to swallow a mouthful of food, but she was very hungry, and the soup was good, a lot better than the thin soup at home. At the first sip of wine a comforting warmth went coursing through her veins, almost a fire, that drove away sad thoughts and restored her spirits.

Rosùte surely would be properly cured in the hospital. The doctor was good, even that woman had told her so. Within fifteen or twenty days at most they would have to come to take her home cured. . . .

The men were chatting. From time to time one would catch hold of the edge of another's jacket and tug it toward himself in order to whisper something into the other's ear as though it were God knows what sort of secret. And instead he was simply saying, 'This year coal isn't worth anything,' or else 'The pigs have been sold at such-and-such a price.' One of them pointing to Mariutine suddenly asked Barbe Zef, 'Is she your daughter?'

And Barbe Zef, 'My niece, orphaned daughter of my brother.'

'Of Gaspari?'

'Of Gaspari.'

'A good-looking *fantate*.'

Then they resumed talking about the weather, cattle, and many other matters that didn't interest Mariutine at all. What did interest and preoccupy her was the considerable number of glasses Barbe Zef gulped down one after the other, and the passing of hours without his taking cognizance of them, without his deciding to get a move on or to set out on the trip back. Could it be that they might have to do that horrible crossing by night? Could it be that Barbe Zef did not remember they had to go back home as soon as possible? . . . She looked at him anxiously, her heart in her mouth, wishing but not daring to make some sort of sign to him, to tell him it was now time to leave.

Then, against her will, her attention wandered. She felt better, the coldness having left her. On the wall opposite her a colorful painting in a lovely gilded frame all at once caught her full attention. It depicted a young man with long blond hair reaching almost to his shoulders. He was dressed in black velvet and wore a great plumed hat. He held around the waist a young woman as beautiful as an angel, with long curls likewise down to her shoulders, dressed in pale blue silk so marvelous that Mariutine had never seen the likes of it before. He was leaning over her to tell her something. But the girl in the painting did not seem pleased. She bent her head with a perplexed and melancholy air. Whatever could the young man in the great plumed hat be telling her? Why was the lovely girl so sad?

At the sides of that painting were photographs of the king and the queen. The queen had a diamond crown on her head and six strands of pearls each bead big as a hazelnut. She too seemed beautiful to Mariutine. The king on the other hand, she liked somewhat less. He was dressed like any ordinary man, only with a ribbon across his chest that didn't signify anything. With that closely cropped hair and moustachios, he seemed especially too old. But maybe she couldn't see well because they were too far away from the light. A pity!

While she was considering these matters, an irresistible sleepiness took hold of her. She had walked so much, she had cried, and now tiredness, the torpor produced by the fire and the wine, weighed down upon her all at once. No matter how she tried to keep her eyes open, they closed. Her head sagged down to her chest. But in dozing the image of Rosùte lying on her stretcher unhappily crossed her thoughts, Rosùte who had disappeared screaming on her way down the long corridor. Mariutine woke up with a start, heaving a deep sigh.

No one paid any attention to her. Barbe Zef and his two friends emptied their glasses and discussed things together gesturing and shaking their fingers at one another. Then all of a sudden they would become silent, interrupting their complicated conversation to stare at their glasses, motionless, with sad eyes. At last Mariutine dozed off to sleep. A tiny black kitten that was rambling around the inn in search of a warm and protected nook leapt lightly into her lap. She hardly felt it; only a mellow soft warmth reached her knees, helping her fall asleep.

She had been napping for a short time when the noise of scraping chairs roused her. Barbe Zef and the other two men were already standing, and they were making ready to leave. They had emptied the entire first bottle and another one too, and they had eaten little or nothing. All three had shining eyes and each wore his hat askew at the top of his head.

'I'm paying,' stammered Barbe Zef rummaging under his shirt to look for the little sack of money.

Mariutine felt sleep and fatigue vanish at once. She opened her eyes wide and was ready to say something, but once again shyness won out and she did not dare. . . . That little bit of cash, that had cost her *mâri* so much toil—yes, they were her mother's coins, from the *mâri*, it was she, poor dear woman, who had earned them dragging herself around through the wide world on her tired feet, and they had given the money to him *when she was dead!*—those coins, held in reserve with so much difficulty, at the price of daily sacrifices, which now were to serve as payment for Rosùte's sickness, and for subsistence until springtime and afterwards too. Now Barbe Zef was setting about squandering them like this . . .

Her heart pounded hard. Although she knew it was dangerous to argue with Barbe Zef when he had been drinking, and although she was ashamed in front of those other two, she worked up courage, and easing around him ever so gently she lightly tugged at his jacket. So lightly did she tug though that he did not understand—or pretended not to understand. He paid, and went out with his buddies by the north side door of the inn leading to

96

the courtyard. Mariutine kept behind him in silence, full of apprehension. Where was he heading, now that it was already almost dark, where was he heading?

There, under the little roof, was a small two-wheeled carriage with its shafts sticking up in the air and a net underneath, one of those that merchants use to transport pigs. The stout man in the short cape entered the stable and came out right away leading a white filly by the halter, the rope harness still on her back. He set about hitching her up. The other, in the great full-length cape, hung back, standing against the wall to take care of some business of his own.

Only then did Barbe Zef seem to remember Mariutine. Rubbing his hands together and really laughing with his mouth and both eyes, he came close to her. In a low voice he announced, 'We've met up with somebody, we have a connection. We can sleep at the farm of this buddy, who owes me some favors.'

The man in the short cape got into the carriage on the right taking hold of the reins and the whip. Barbe Zef got in on the other side and pushed Mariutine to the center. The man in the full cape remained standing stiffly against the wall with his legs apart. At the door the hostess appeared with the babe in her arms, and she taught the little fellow to wave his small hand in goodbye.

The white filly moved on.

PART THREE

*T*he road ran due north, and the snow which covered it had in a few hours become as hard and slick as a slab of glass. Nevertheless the white filly, shod with iron cleats and knowing that they were on the way home, trotted gaily along shaking the fur-trimmed harness and harness bells.

Along the way, listening to the men as they spoke, Mariutine had come to understand that the fellow who was driving them was Compare Àgnul, master of the Case Rotte, the one whose cow and calf Barbe Zef had saved. The discovery had pleased and reassured her, as if it implied a long-standing acquaintanceship for her, too.

In fact, hardly had the little carriage debarked in the courtyard of the farm, when the first person to greet them was the shepherd boy whom they had met that night on the mountain. He had filled out and become taller. He had a fine pair of new clogs, and upon seeing Mariutine and Barbe Zef, he blushed and turned his head to look elsewhere, pretending not to recognize them. Then he quickly got busy unhitching the filly.

Compare Àgnul's dairy farm compared favorably with the loveliest farmsteads that Mariutine had seen in the plain. The house was built partly of stone and partly of wood, as is customary in the mountains, but it was commodious and almost new, with a pretty gallery that went all around the upper story. Beside it, on one side was a low shed crowded with carts and equipment, and on the other the hayloft and the stables. A vast courtyard stretched out in front of the house.

A huge dog came leaping up around the carriage, barking in joyous welcome. From the homestead and from the stables, drawn by the hubbub, the youngest of the children came forth, but at seeing two new persons, they halted timidly at a distance. Other more grown up children, on the contrary, who had been ice skating on a frozen-over ditch, drew near, self-confident and curious, clustering around the newcomers.

Everybody knew Barbe Zef, and they were as used to seeing him turn up unexpectedly as to seeing rain fall from the sky. Whether with his sack of coal on his back or for other business, they were used to him, but who ever was that *fantate,* and what had brought her there?

A young girl ran into the house to spread the news. And suddenly Compare Àgnul's wife and sister-in-law, two good-looking buxom women, appeared at the kitchen door; then little by little they moved forward into the courtyard. And behind them came also three beautiful girls of from fifteen to eighteen years of age.

Mariutine, feeling herself the object of general curiosity, shrank back awkwardly into her shawl and would have wished to become ever so small, to utterly disappear so as to avoid their glances. Despite the piercing cold, she felt all flushed, and she didn't know where to rest her eyes without meeting the eyes of others fixed on her. Above all, the attention of the three girls intimidated her, the girls who from behind the women peered over their mother's shoulders craning their necks the better to observe Mariutine. One of them, who looked like a boy, with a little headful of short dark curls, was laughing, perhaps without malice; but that laugh of hers increased Mariutine's discomfort.

In the midst of so many new faces, the girl clung to

Barbe Zef as to an anchor of safety, and she sought to attach herself as firmly as possible to his garments, but Barbe Zef was joking and darting around here and there as if he were unable to keep still. The cold air and the ride in the carriage had cleared his head from his touch of inebriation, and he recognized everybody. He joyously greeted women and children, calling them by name as though he were a member of the family. Because of the well-deserved praise acquired through helping with the cow and her calf, and sure of a hearty welcome, he had assumed an air of importance and authority.

It was Compare Àgnul who remembered Mariutine, who had remained alone on the side with lowered eyes, feeling a full measure of cold and inferiority. And with two words he brought his wife up-to-date about who she was.

The news spread rapidly from mouth to mouth: 'She's the niece of Barbe Zef. She's the niece of Barbe Zef.'

And at once the women left off staring to take her in amongst themselves. The girls too, their curiosity satisfied, welcomed her cordially.

Barbe Zef wanted to go to the stable to see *his calf,* which, said Compare Àgnul, was on the way to becoming a fine beef cow.

The women accompanied Mariutine to the kitchen so that she could warm herself a bit.

The kitchen was low and smoky, and in the middle of it on the great circular free-standing *focolare* blazed a fire of bundled dried branches and twigs. On the broad grills placed over the embers twenty or so pork chops gave off a savory appetizing aroma.

'This year, for the pigsticking, we had to do the job without Barbe Zef,' said the farmwife to Mariutine, casting an uneasy glance at a burning pork chop and pulling it back hastily from the fire. 'Too much snow to risk going all the way up to your place to call him. You did well to come down.'

'Don't you want to take off your shawl? Come closer to the flames; you're all frozen,' one of the girls commented kindly.

'What's your name?' asked the other, the one who looked like a boy. 'Mariùte? . . . I am Ursule, and these are my sisters, Teresine and Catinùte.'

Beside the fire, curled up in a big arm chair on casters, sat a very very old man, so tiny, wizened, and dried out as to seem hardly taller and heavier than an infant. He was dozing with his head on his breast and his hands on his knees; by the light of the fire his bald head shone like polished ivory, and from his toothless mouth a trickle of saliva flowed down his chin.

'Ninety-six years . . . ' murmured the housewife pointing him out to Mariutine. 'He can't walk any longer, and he's brought here in the morning and not taken away until he goes to bed. He sleeps all day long.'

Outside it was beginning to get dark, and one after another the babies and children began to file into the kitchen and assemble around the fire. This one took the cat on his knees, that one pulled the dog's tail, another collided in passing with the legs of the great-grandfather, who opened wide his astonished pale eyes, and at once closed them again to resume sleeping.

Amongst the children there was one of fourteen years or so, brunette and of ruddy complexion, with a fur cap on his head, who seemed invested with the office of monitor, the distributor of smacks on the head. And he discharged his mission with maximum zeal. If the housewife said to someone, 'Move over, you bother me,' at once that fellow hastened over in dead earnest to smack the troublemaker's head. There were shrieks and little brawls in which the dog too participated, barking and siding with this one or that.

There was an endless procession of children. They were of all different ages: one in swaddling clothes in a servant girl's arms, others already adolescent and almost full-grown men, for Compare Àgnul lived in his homestead together with two brothers, and he had seven sons of his own and his brother had eight sons and daughters, a fine family of healthy young people, without counting the servants and the shepherd boys.

On the *focolare* in an enormous cauldron bubbled the *jote,* the characteristic soup made of different kinds of flours and assorted vegetables, and the girls were coming and going with plates and glasses, diligent about setting the table, while the housewife had taken down a smoked ham from where it was hanging by a rope, to make a celebration in honor of the guests.

She was just beginning to slice it when at the door there was heard the scraping and yelping of the dogs followed by a noise of heavy footsteps and clomping shoes. The door was flung open and the other two masters of the house came in.

One, Compare Vigiùt, was a big strapping burly fellow, still youthful, tall and broad, with a full high-complexioned good-natured face, and in his voice, in his speech and gestures he resembled his brother Àgnul so much that one could have been taken for the other. The other brother, who must have been the eldest of the three, by one of those anomalies not infrequent among peasant families, did not resemble anyone. He seemed to be of another race entirely, and he was a hunchback both in front and behind, dark-skinned as a cricket, with a short round cape on his shoulders, and on his head a bizarre pointed hat.

He came in blowing his nose into a red handkerchief and sending forth a long blast similar to that of a horn. He got rid of his cape, kept the hat on, and sat down beside the *focolare* extending his hands and legs to the flames. The children crowded around him. The housewife began to ladle out the soup.

The hunchback had two small, intensely lively eyes set quite close together, and he spoke in a high-pitched voice. He talked a lot and laughed even more, gesticulating freely with his long arms. Mariutine at first thought he was a bit feeble minded, or that he was playing the clown, but it did not take her long to realize that the truth was quite different.

In fact, if officially Compare Àgnul played the role of head of the family, in reality the true and only master was the hunchback. It was he who, orphaned at age sixteen together with his brothers, had known how to manage so well that from nothing he had accumulated almost a fortune. Thanks to him, the three brothers were now considered among the major businessmen of those parts and they owned, besides that beautiful homestead, a hundred head of cattle, and woods and grazing grounds on the mountainsides. From the special attentions the housewife paid to him, from the deference with which everyone listened to him, it was obvious that the hunchback was the head and soul of the whole enterprise. It was he who held the reins of everything in his hands and made all the decisions. His brothers, although they were by now in their fifties, remained completely under his authority and at his orders, and when they went to the markets to buy and sell wholesale, they were no more than the instruments of the decisions of Compare Guerrino, who ventured away from the house only two or three times a month to go down to the city or to visit the more important fairs. He must have been good and merry too, for the children had a tremendous familiarity with him and sought out his company.

Mariutine, amidst all the comings and goings of new people who kept entering, among all those voices and that laughter, in that hubbub of individuals linked together by kinship or by long association who were engaging in conversations in which she could not join, who were laughing about things that she didn't know and didn't understand, felt herself a stranger, disoriented and out of place.

Here was Barbe Zef returning from the stables with Compare Àgnul. . . . But what did she care, after all, about Barbe Zef? He came into the kitchen winking his eye, rubbing his hands, greedily and cheerfully eyeing the laid table. He felt not in the least embarrassed. It was as though he had lived in that house for a hundred years. He did not even seem to remember her existence. Behind Barbe Zef came Compare Àgnul in his short cape with the hareskin collar. He took it off, hanging it on its nail behind the door, and he also took off the green scarf that he wore around his neck; and he came in thrusting forth his paunch, on which shone a large gold chain. Compare Vigiùt, who was hard of hearing and took little part in the conversation, was balancing two of the tots on his knees, one on each leg, bouncing them up and down.

Now even the girls had abandoned Mariutine because they had to help the housewife ladle out the *jote,* and bit by bit she had moved away from the *focolare* in order not to stand in the way. She had drawn back against the wall into a shadowy corner, almost hidden by the high credenza, where one or another of the dogs came from time to time to nuzzle her skirts suspiciously.

The dogs were three in number. Strange to say, the two that belonged to Compare Àgnul and Compare Vigiùt vaguely resembled their masters in the shape of their heads, in their reddish-brown coats, and in their heavy and clumsy movements. And likewise Compare Guerrino's dog, a wretched and excitable mongrel, with the elongated muzzle of a marten and small sparkling eyes set close together, was a striking portrait of the hunchback, resembling him as son to father. The dog stayed sitting on his hind legs next to his master, with his neck straining, his unmoving eye intent on him, and when the hunchback, without interrupting what he was saying and without looking at the animal, would pass his hand over the dog's lean back with its visible vertebrae, the dog twitched with recognition.

Yes, in this household even the dogs had someone who loved them a little. . . . A great melancholy took hold of Mariutine, a melancholy that was perhaps fatigue, and with it came a sharp homesickness for her cabin lost in the midst of the snow; for Rosùte who loved her; for her sheep—they at least knew her; for Petòti, who in winter's long nights, almost feeling their isolation, used to rub his nose against her knees, looking at her with human eyes.

So many times, so many other times, one might say ever since infancy, she had found herself in just such a situation, arriving by chance amid strange people who welcomed her under their roof, who gave her the charity of a piece of bread. Yet she had never before felt such isolation and such melancholy. But then there had been the *mâri* . . . her *mâri:* taciturn, unsociable, her face hard and severe, and nevertheless in the shadow of her love Mariutine had felt protected and secure as with no one else in the world. Her *mâri,* Rosùte . . .

What an abundance, what bounty in that house! Here too one was in the mountains. Here too, outside, all around, there was cold, silence, deep snow; but no one noticed it, no one seemed to remember it. . . . How many good-looking children, healthy and lucky! . . . One of them was about the same age as Rosùte. A little girl in a red dress resembled her somewhat. . . . What was her poor little Rosùte doing at that moment? If she had only been there too with everyone else, to enjoy that fine fire, those good foods laid out on the table, that sense of well-being for which, however much it was dimmed by an obscure suffering, Mariutine felt almost guilty!

Perhaps from the other end of the kitchen the hunchback with his keen eyes was aware of her melancholy, for he got up with a jerk from the bench where he had been sitting, and with two steps of his long legs he was near her.

'If she thinks I'm worthy of her,' he declaimed with his sharp voice in falsetto, making a great exaggerated bow, 'she'll come with me, the fair maiden—the most beautiful!' And taking her by the hand with his arm held high, as though they were starting to dance the monferrina, he escorted her to the table and made her sit beside him to his right. His action and his voice were so funny that even Mariutine began to laugh. A salvo of handclapping burst out, and with a scraping and scrambling all took their places around the steaming soup plates.

*

The great-grandfather in his wheelchair was pushed close beside the table.

In the country, among agricultural families, rules of hierarchy are followed rigorously, and the old man's habitual place was that given to Mariutine, to the right of the master of the house.

One of the girls tucked the table napkin under his chin, crumbled the bread, and poured him a bit of wine mixed with water. He was now completely awake, and with hostile persistence he fixed his eyes, strangely live and mobile in the bloodless visage, on the unknown female who had taken his place. But he diverted them from her immediately as soon as his soup was put in front of him. They served him last, the better to be able to watch over him while he was eating, for he had the habit of swallowing pieces so large that he risked strangulation. That day too he began to swallow spoonful after spoonful of the thick *jote* with such greediness that the food immediately began to go down the wrong way.

'Slowly, grandpa,' the housewife shouted into his ear thumping him with little smacks on the back. 'Come on, nobody's running after you. What's your rush?' and she wiped his mouth and chin as one does with babies. The old man at once began to eat again, impatient. The hand that brought the tablespoon to his mouth was as bony as that of a skeleton, with large veins that looked like ropes, and it trembled so hard that at every spoonful half of the oily broth spilled over his chin and napkin, which instantly turned all yellow from it.

Although he had been the last to start eating, he was the first one finished. Then he began to turn his restless eyes toward the courses to follow and to peer suspiciously into the plates of the others. Taking advantage of a momentary lapse in the housewife's attention, after having furtively glanced around to make sure that no one was watching, little by little he reached out his hand to pull toward himself a large roll of bread. He grasped it and with uncommon slyness hid it under his jacket.

The hunchback meanwhile was full of solicitude and attentiveness toward Mariutine. Whether because of his good-natured temperament, or because he liked having that fresh young face beside him, he put into play all the wiles he knew to cheer up his guest and put her at ease. Obviously he already knew the reason for the Zef family's trip and about the meeting with Compare Àgnul, but he asked her hardly anything about her little sister. Nor did he show that he had noticed her melancholy. He was trying his best to distract her and divert her with other things, different thoughts, and meanwhile he put the choicest bits on her plate and continually refilled her glass with a sparkling light white wine that seemed made expressly for reviving the dead.

'Good cheer, be merry everyone, for it's carnival time!'

He too drank a lot, and with drinking he became more and more talkative. He tossed off jokes, he made up stories, he accompanied his speech with anecdotes and proverbs that made the whole table roll with laughter. And between one round of buffoonery and the next, he turned his shining eyes and his red-tipped ears gallantly toward Mariutine, and he told her about the relationships within his extended family. He told her the names and ages of the various members and brought her up to date about the accomplishments of the little children and the pranks of the big ones.

'You see?' he said, pointing to the boy with the fur cap at the far end of the table, who was the dispenser of smacks to the head, and who was all intent on a large pork chop, 'That one there, we call him the Praetor.'

'Praetor! Praetor! Praetor!' shrilled the little ones on all sides; and the Praetor, who had his mouth full, this time didn't move, but continued to chew imperturbably, with his eyes on his plate.

At first the girl listened absentmindedly. Then, gradually, without intending it, she became more attentive, even amused. Little by little she felt her impression of being alone and lost amid strange people vanish: through the words of her neighbor, the world around her began to be interesting, and the food, the wine, the warmth, and the contact with other young people gave her a sort of physical drunkenness, an amazed bewilderment.

She hadn't eaten her fill—really eaten her fill—for a long time. At home, she used to pretend that she had no appetite or that she had eaten earlier. She fibbed in order to give what little there was and the better tidbits to Rosùte and Barbe Zef. Here, the housewife continually passed her the platter so that she might serve herself. The hunchback insisted that she drink. Mariutine resisted weakly. She stole glances of naive desire at the luscious slices of pink ham, thick, piled high on the cutting-board, and at the transparent wine, pale blond like her hair, in the large flowered jug, and she hadn't the strength to refuse. The woman and the man kept refilling plate and glass generously.

Before such overflowing abundance she felt confused

111

and ashamed. She feared especially that Teresine, Ursule, and Catinùte, the girls, would notice the mountain of stuff she had let be put on her plate and would judge her to be greedy. But the girls had other things to do than pay attention to her, one busy helping the servant girl bring plates and jugs to the table and take them away again, the other two feeding the tots and infants at the foot of the table. The only one who spied on her plate was the old man, his eyes full of envy between inflamed, lashless eyelids.

Under this persistent stare, Mariutine blushed, bent her head, and began to eat with deliberate slowness. It seemed to her that the hunger she had endured could be read on her face. Nevertheless soon she managed to forget even the old man and his spiteful eyes.

An unconscious need for life, for freedom from cares, for joy invaded her entire being. Although she was not yet completely free of her embarrassment and did not dare retort to the wisecracks of the hunchback and laugh over them as did the others, her vivacious eyes spoke and laughed for her. They rested with curiosity and trust on the merry faces surrounding her.

Flushed, overheated, a bit overwrought, she broke out on her forehead in little drops of sweat like pearls under the blond hair. From time to time she had the impression that between herself and the others a light vaporous fog arose—but perhaps it was just the savory fumes of the last pork chops that were getting done on the grill—and that she could no longer tell people apart, remembering only that they were relatives, from the same stock. She was struck by the fact that all, young and old, had one characteristic feature in common, something in the face: the eyes, perhaps, so near the base of the nose, round and shining? . . . And in a flash, she had the impression that she was sitting in the midst of a long table of monkeys, and the vision seemed to her so funny that she began to laugh quietly all by herself, hiding her face in her napkin.

'What good people! Welcoming, not stuck up, a bit conceited maybe over their easy circumstances and eager to make a show of them, but is that a defect, really? Better to be like this, than stingy and greedy,' thought Mariutine.

From time to time her eyes went by chance toward Barbe Zef, who, seated between Compare Àgnul and Compare Vigiùt, was eating voraciously and drinking like a fish, and then the memory and the reality of the life that she would have to resume the next day went through her mind, but each time more fleet and faded, always more remote, and it was her same will now that drove those thoughts away and pushed them back. Her fifteen years simply refused to dwell upon them, for she was tired of suffering, eager for joy, all absorbed in the beautiful animated and radiant spectacle that shone before her.

'Eat, little one,' Compare Guerrino told her, passing without ceremony to the familiar form of speech, and putting on her plate a *martondella,* a meatball made of pork liver, wrapped in a net of meat fat.

'No, no, enough, I can't,' rejoined the girl, beginning to laugh.

Now she was laughing at every little thing. Everything seemed to her so odd, so amusing, that she could not manage to stay serious. It was like a wave that little by little overcame her, bearing her away, submerging her. She couldn't explain it. She only laughed, and when she was not actually laughing, she felt the urge to laugh.

Auff, how warm it was with that fire of bundled sticks and all these people! . . . Compare Vigiùt had taken off his jacket and though it was well into January, he was sitting at the table in shirtsleeves. How funny he was, Compare Vigiùt! . . . He was the most conceited and the stupidest of the brothers, and to be all the more admired by the Zefs, he treated them with a certain superciliousness. He gave himself airs and, when he opened his mouth, with the piercing voice of the deaf, it was to brag about his wealth. Mariutine could hardly restrain herself from laughing in his face. The hunchback on the other hand, while supper was coming to an end, became more intimate and almost tender with the girl beside him.

'You see, my beauty,' he said, indicating his brother Vigiùt with a subtle nod, 'that poor man there, he's younger than I am . . . you have to scream to make yourself heard. He has lost one of his five senses. But I say that he lost it before he even had it. Five senses! . . . They say that man is born with five senses. But some are born with three, with two; and few, very few, with all five intact. It's all a question of this, this, this,' and he knocked his forehead with his knuckles.

While speaking, he placed his hand on the girl's arm, punctuating his words with little nudges of his elbow. There was no hint that he was hot. On the contrary he was almost deadly pale; only his ears were red and his eyes shining, lit up, sharp, and he was wearing that funny peaked hat on his head.

Two or three times it seemed to Mariutine that under the table his long legs were seeking out hers, and inch by inch she drew her feet back under her chair, suddenly intimidated. But there was no time to speculate over this nonsense. The boys, unseen by their mothers, had put chestnuts in the ashes, which all at once popped up into the air with an explosion like a gunshot.

'Get out of there, you rascals,' hollered Compare Àgnul, and the Praetor went on duty again, pursuing the guilty ones and pushing them out toward the barn.

'Bau, bau!' went the dogs, but they too laughed with gaping mouths on hanging jaws.

The younger woman of the house, mother of the three girls, had withdrawn to a corner of the kitchen to nurse the lastborn baby at her breast. At the end of the big table, two stalwart fellows three or four years old, wearing characteristic broad pants of green felt, had fallen asleep both at the same time, their heads on the tablecloth, as two ripe pears fall to the ground when attached to the same stem.

'Who took my bread?' the older woman of the house asked in a severe tone. 'I hadn't even touched it yet.'

She began to search in the old man's deep pockets. She found the bread and took it back from him. He remained staring at her with half-shut eyes as though he could not understand. Then suddenly he began to cry with his chin on his chest, in a faint childlike and plaintive whining.

'Oh give him back the bread, Celeste!' exclaimed the hunchback. 'He can't eat it anyway, and tonight we don't want any complaints.'

*

While Compare Guerrino authoritatively pronounced these words, the lively harmonies of an accordion were beginning to be heard. Ursule, Teresine, and Catinùte leapt up and ran to open the door. A comical-looking group burst in, jumping and dancing their way into the kitchen.

There were five or six players in masks obviously homemade but meant to be scary or grotesque. One was fiery red and with charcoal markings, and it was meant to represent the devil. A second one consisted of an extremely long nose protruding above an equally long raggedy beard of coarse fibers. A third one had a pig's snout. The others in the troupe had been content with sticking a colored rag or a piece of paper fringe onto their everyday clothes, or simply turning their jackets inside out and putting nightcaps on their heads.

The devil vaulted about like a young stag. The old man walked on his hands with his head down and his legs in the air. As for the pig, he sang crowing cock-a-doodle-doo with the voice of a rooster.

They were youths from the neighboring farms, habitual visitors of the *filò*, and probably rivals amongst themselves for the girls, linked by the common desire to 'cele-brate carnival time.'

The merry party was led by a slim blond fellow without a mask, a bit lame, calm and collected, who had a fine accordion with painted decorations slung across his shoulders. With a vigorous pulling out of the bellows, he launched into a dancing tune and the cue for a song.

It was a magnificent success. And since supper was finished anyway, everyone, except the two older men and Barbe Zef intent on draining the last wine from a jug, quit the kitchen and amid laughing remarks and applause moved out into the barn with the new arrivals.

The barn was newly whitewashed, roomy, and well tended. Thirty or so reddish-brown cows with albino eyes, small but with sleek hides, populated it along with their numerous calves, and they spread throughout its interior a rather moist and heavy warmth. Along the walls narrow wooden benches, a few rough-hewn tables, and some chairs had been prepared for the *filò*. The lighting, consisting of two old kerosene lanterns hung from the ceiling, was not excessively bright, but the company made do with it.

Before everyone could find a suitable place to stand or sit—and in the company that he or she preferred—there was a moment of confusion and jostling during which the hunchback, with the pretext of escorting her, was at Mariutine's heels rubbing up against her as much as he could. He squeezed her elbow, he touched her arm, and with a blade of straw he tickled her on the neck, but as though by accident and without ulterior motive, eyeing her as though inadvertently out of the corner of his eye.

And all at once, above the uproar, there resounded a blast of nose blowing, long and penetrating like the summons blared out by a hunting horn.

'Make way! Make way!' he set up a shrill shout, with his sharp voice in falsetto.

At once the crowd drew back along the walls, and the accordion player lit into a spirited mazurka. Compare Guerrino, tossing his hat in the air and catching hold of the young girl's waist, went spinning off into the middle of the little crowd of spectators. Although for a hunchback he was strangely tall and very long legged, his head hardly came up as high as Mariutine's breast, and yet he lifted her almost up into the air and whirled her around so dizzily that it seemed as though her feet never touched the ground.

They danced the famous 'toe and heel' mazurka, in great esteem in that part of the countryside, with its intricate steps and innumerable variations. Mariutine had had virtually no opportunities to dance it, but she danced by instinct like most of the mountain girls once she had overcome her initial shyness, and she rushed ahead confident and light on her feet, gracefully following her partner. He, gripping her like a spider, 'led' her in masterful style, with the trippings, turns, and virtuosities of a consummate artist. He stamped his heel, throwing up his foot shod in a kind of shoe that passed for citified, the toe pointed upward. He opened his legs like a compass and closed them again with a click. His humped back was of no trouble to him, nor did the years seem to weigh on him, for he could not have been less than fifty or fifty-five years old. The tails of his jacket flew out, matched in the same rhythms by the fluttering out of Mariutine's smock and skirts.

The company had abruptly withdrawn its attention from the masked entertainers to focus on the dancing. At every tricky step, at every unexpected and original variation, a murmur of approval arose, and some enthusiast couldn't help exclaiming, 'They're neat, by gosh! They're neat!'

When at last, with a full and throbbing chord, the mazurka came to an end, they all clapped their hands. A shepherd boy brought the hunchback his hat, in which he had stuck a long rooster feather, a sign of primacy, and the cry 'Music! Music!' resounded on all sides.

At once the devil with his fiery red, ugly face, the old man with the long white beard, and the fellow with the pig's snout who had given up his cock-a-doodle-doo, with great seriousness, knowing that they had an obligation to dance well, took Ursule, Teresine, and Catinùte out onto the dance floor. They began to wheel about in rhythm with the music, in their heavy hobnailed shoes.

Meanwhile Compare Guerrino had not let go of Mariutine, and he urged her with great familiarity towards a corner of the barn where there was a low stool. Panting and out of breath, he wiped the sweat dripping down his forehead with a large red kerchief. Mariutine too was overheated. One of her braids had come loose, and her heart was beating as after a fast race. Yet she felt happy and proud of her well-earned success. Nor did it ever enter her mind to regret having had an older, hunchbacked partner instead of a handsome young man. She took her place cheerily enough beside Compare Guerrino, and she smiled at him gratefully.

They were silent for a bit. A cluster of people separated them like a wall from the space allotted to dancing. No one paid attention to them. Only two white calves from their place close by turned around to look at them placidly. Finally the hunchback, continuing to pass the kerchief over his deadly pale and sweaty face, without looking at his companion said nonchalantly, 'You can't be all that well off up there in that hole where you live. Why don't you find a job in town?'

The question touched a spot too sensitive for Mariutine, excited by the dance and by all the extraordinary events of that whole day though she was, to hear it calmly. She suddenly felt whisked away from the joy and heedlessness of the moment and brought back to the dark foreboding that had made up the fear and menace of her entire life. She started up and blushed furiously; nevertheless, by a great effort conquering her bashfulness, she answered: 'I'd rather have a hard time up there at our place, than go be a servant . . . ' she murmured with lowered eyes, but firmly. 'And then, even if I wanted to, I couldn't.'

'Why couldn't you?'

'I have to take care of Barbe and my sister.'

The hunchback laughed. 'As for Barbe, he's old enough to look out for himself. But what do you mean . . . your sister! . . . How old is she?'

'She's going on seven.'

'And where is she now?'

He seemed to have forgotten Rosùte's tragedy completely.

'At the hospital in Forni. We brought her there this morning, but she'll soon be cured and she'll be released.'

'Ah, ah, she'll be released . . . ,' repeated the hunchback two or three times as if he were talking to himself. 'She'll be released.'

And after a long pause, he continued breezily, 'In town, my dear, in the evening, hundreds and hundreds of lights go on all by themselves as though by a miracle, and at night it's as bright as by day. Down there people don't trudge along as we do up here in the midst of snow stones and crags, but they walk on streets smooth as velvet, and, if it rains, they take shelter beneath the porticoes. In town there is music in the square at least twice a week, and people go to the movies and the theater. At carnival time they dance on a platform all festooned with artificial flowers and many-colored balloons, and hundreds of maskers, not scraggly like these, but splendid ones dressed in silk and velvet, offer sugar almonds to the pretty girls.'

And since Mariutine proved interested despite herself and turned her wide-open ingenuous eyes to him in utter fascination, he continued.

'Think about it beautiful,' he said in a low and insinuating voice. 'Why don't you want to try it? . . . And, if ever you do, remember Compare Guerrino. I have occasion to go down to town two or three times a month, and I have many connections. We could find a respectable family, that would treat you as a daughter. . . . Or perhaps a lady living alone, or better yet, a widower or an elderly bachelor. . . . A master is always less fussy and demanding than a mistress. I might even know of somebody just right for you. . . . Such a person, you see, would be someone safe for you to rely on. He wouldn't treat you badly. The one I have in mind knows what young people need. Is that clear? . . . If ever you feel like doing it, just let me know somehow. And meanwhile think about it. Will you do that?'

'You're very kind, Compare Guerrino, and I don't know how to thank you . . . ' murmured the confused girl. 'As for thinking about it, I will do that, you can be sure, but, as I've told you . . . '

'Ta ta ta,' the hunchback interrupted her sharply. 'I've just been telling you these things for the sake of saying them. You have to have something to talk about. By the way, how old are you?'

'Fifteen.'

'That's young. You look at least four years older. You already have such breasts! While dancing I felt them, you know? And what a sweet scent you have—really of a fresh rose, or a musk rose.'

As he made these remarks Compare Guerrino's tongue licked his lips and he looked at the girl hungrily. His eyes lingered on her budding breasts that were still lightly heaving, on her thighs that could be readily guessed at as they were outlined under her thin skirt, and on her red and fleshy mouth.

'You're the most beautiful *fantate* I've ever seen,' he murmured, pressing against her on the low stool.

Mariutine blazed up in blushes. She felt diffident toward the hunchback because he was her elder and because he was the master, and even if she had known how, she would not have dared to reply, for her extreme poverty had shaped in her ever since early childhood the habit of compliance and almost of servility with regard to anyone outside of her own family. But these were the first praises, the first compliments ever, that had come to her coarsely directed toward her physical self. More than flattering her, they caused her deep embarrassment, just as did Compare Guerrino's speeches and familiarity, which while they interested and amused her, also aroused an obscure sense of discomfort.

Just then, abruptly raising her eyes as though summoned by other eyes, she met the gaze of Barbe Zef, who had entered unannounced into the barn. Crouched on his heels next to a table where they were gambling, behind a cluster of people, he was eying Mariutine and her companion closely. On meeting the girl's gaze, he swiftly shifted his eyes and pretended to be following the game. Mariutine had noticed the whole scene, but she did not make anything of it. And the hunchback too perhaps had noticed, for, without paying any further attention to her and without a word of goodbye, he got up and left his place with an indifferent air.

Joining the people who made up the *filò*, lingering first with this one and then with the other, tossing off a joke here, a compliment there, and a sardonic word further on, distributing to the shepherd boys little tweaks of the ear and to the girls fond little pinches, like a king holding court he passed the entire company in review. Swarthy, unattractive, and deformed as he was, he nevertheless had the manner of the true master, and in his eyes there was an astute and intelligent expression. When he reached Barbe Zef, he turned to him with a joke, and Barbe Zef replied quietly and with deference, without the remotest trace of awkwardness. Then Compare Guerrino, at the center of a small circle of men, tight lipped and without laughing, began to tell a story, spicy certainly and bold, for Barbe Zef and the other older men, already leering after the glasses of wine they had drunk, could be seen splitting their sides with laughter.

Meanwhile the young men of the family and after them the other youths, as soon as they saw Mariutine free from Compare Guerrino's escort, rushed to invite her to dance. And she, her eyes agleam like two blue pearls, rosy and disheveled, passed from one to the next, light on her feet and radiant with joy.

The dancers kept it up until nearly midnight, when, inexplicably, there was a sudden pause and a silence. Then without need for a word of agreement, men women and children, and even the white-haired old men, all bounded up on their feet at the same time, and unfurling their voices they joined in a chorus:

The sun at sunset is a glory
And the moon splendid above
And the stars they form a crown
And sweethearts are making love.

It was the traditional chorus that concluded the *filò*. But even apart from that, the shepherd boys who were falling asleep, the platters of chestnuts where nothing more remained than the shells, the empty pitchers, and the languishing conversations were other signs all of which clearly indicated that the evening was over.

The visitors, led by the lame accordionist, were saying their good-byes. Since Barbe Zef and Mariutine would have to be leaving the next day at dawn to make the return journey to their high land, the thanks and leave-takings of the family were exchanged on the spot before everybody disbanded to go to bed.

Ursule invited Mariutine to sleep with them in their

bed. Barbe Zef had a good pallet and a heavy blanket in the barn. The others, after innumerable '*mandis*' and handclasps, went off on their own.

In the little bedroom, the girls quickly got undressed, while through the nocturnal silence the drawn-out tones of the receding accordion continued to reach their ears:

Oh my dearest Ursuline,
Oh my dusky darling one,
Black your curls and sweet your mouth,
Created just for making love.

The next morning Mariùte, in the darkness and with her shoes in hand in order not to disturb the others, tiptoed down the stairs and stepped out into the court-yard. It was dawn. At the discreet sound of her footsteps, the dogs, without leaving their kennels, numbed from the freezing hours of night, did no more than let out a snarl and a whimper. At that moment Barbe Zef emerged from the barn.

All was white and motionless. Over the countryside there reigned the silence of isolation in the snow.

With a regretful glance Mariutine lifted her eyes to the sleeping farmstead. She had left Teresine and Catinùte deep in sleep, but while she was getting ready to leave the room, Ursule had lifted herself on her elbow, with her eyes still shut, and had said to her, 'Give me a kiss.' Then she had let herself fall back and she was again asleep. Sweet Ursule, the best and the dearest of all.

Barbe Zef, taciturn and bundled up into his cloak, and Mariutine, wrapped with her shawl drawn up to her eyes, crossed the courtyard and were hurrying to pass through the gate when the pandemonium of the dogs suddenly halted them. The cold forgotten, the dogs had this time leapt from their kennels into the middle of the courtyard with high barking; but they were not menacing barks. On the contrary, they were festive and affectionate. The next moment the two travelers understood the reason for that behavior.

From the main part of the house, Compare Guerrino was hastily emerging, and with three steps of his long legs he had crossed the white space that separated them. He must have dressed in a great hurry, for his pants were hardly fastened, his short round cape was all twisted on his shoulders. But the inseparable pointed hat was poised on the top of his head. There was plenty of light even though it was still nighttime. The hunchback was carrying under his arm a fat package tied crosswise with string. In the freezing air, he was green in the face, and appeared thinner and older.

'Hey hey, friend, so is this how you sneak away?' he called jovially, tapping Barbe Zef's paunch in mock reproof. 'And with nothing to put your teeth into on the road? Come, come,' he continued thrusting the package into Mariutine's hands—who, all confused, was defensively drawing back. 'Empty sacks can't stand up. At this time of day and in this rotten weather, don't bother to stand on ceremony. Listen, *ninine,* don't let it break,' he added, fixing her with his close, sparkling eyes. 'Have a good trip, and so long!'

And having said that, with two leaps like a grasshopper he had recrossed the courtyard, reached the doorway from which he had come, and disappeared.

✳

For the entire journey Barbe Zef went on ahead of Mariutine without addressing a word to her. Only once, at a stretch of road that was hard going, did he turn brusquely to say, 'Mind that you don't drop the bundle.'

And another time, even more brusquely, 'Give that bundle to me.'

The road was most arduous and Mariutine, relieved of the parcel but exhausted by the exertion and by the powerful emotions of the previous day, and having slept little, trudged on through the snow with an effort that was almost pain. She was nevertheless doing her best not to let herself be outdistanced by Barbe Zef, who evidently, even if he was not concerned about her, was concerned about getting home before nightfall. The cold was so stinging that breath, as soon as it left the mouth, condensed and formed icicles that stuck in thin frozen fringes to Barbe Zef's moustache and on the shawl Mariutine had tightly wrapped around her head and neck.

Mariutine desperately needed to swallow down something that might warm her. But since Barbe Zef, with as little need for refreshment as a camel, was forging ahead without touching food or drink, she did not dare to ask him for anything. They had been walking for just two hours but it seemed to her that they had been on the road forever. What worried her almost more than hunger and fatigue was the fear that Barbe Zef for lack of landmarks was heading in a direction which, even if it wasn't totally mistaken, would prolong the journey.

She recognized Mount Orticello and Mount Tiàrfin, which the light of dawn tinged with a pale pink. But where was that tree half split by lightning that had stood out the day before, contorted and grotesque in the midst of the snow? Where were the stumps of Bosco Tagliato? . . . To return to their glen they absolutely had to cross through it. Might Barbe Zef, experienced in mountain lore like few other local people, have deliberately chosen another route because it was more manageable, or might he himself, despite his experience, have blundered?

At this doubt Mariutine felt tears almost come to her eyes, for her swollen feet, stiff and aching in the huge soaked shoes, refused to continue the journey. Only the fear that if she stopped Barbe Zef might abandon her on the mountain, and an awareness of mortal danger, prevented her from pausing to rest.

Just then suddenly . . . when she had concluded that

certainly they were off the right track, and, at the risk of offending her uncle, was about to tell him so, just then suddenly, in the totally motionless silence that smothered every voice—a voice!

It seems to come from far off, from very far off. . . . It is a drawn-out and impassioned lament. . . . But it is not a human voice. It is the yelping and crying of Petòti, who has been waiting for them, and who has not left off calling them and crying all day and all night! And he is still at it, all over again. Closer; clearer; and here he is, no longer distressed, but excited, quivering with hope, crazed with joy, for the faithful companion has heard his masters' footsteps coming nearer in the snow, and he is greeting them!

And then unexpectedly, as at the touch of a magic wand, there in front of their eyes is the hut with its high crest of snow, its little barred windows, its shed with its square wooden shingles covered with bark.

*

Barbe Zef opened the door. Petòti hurled himself to meet them like a creature possessed, leaping howling and contorting himself. The man carefully lowered his pack onto the table and without delay went out again and returned with a bundle of wood which he stacked in the fireplace. He came and went swiftly without showing any sign of weariness. He lit the fire, and with his pocketknife he cut the cord which had tied up the package of provisions. One by one with meticulous attention he drew forth and set out on the table the good things that were presents from Compare Guerrino: a sausage, some thick slices of ham, a small mold of çuc, besides the bread and a piece of pizza with bits of bacon. Finally there was a great bottle of greenish glass that looked full of water, so clear and transparent were its contents.

Before deciding to place it on the table next to everything else, Barbe Zef weighed it at arm's length, shook it, and examined it doubtfully against the light. The bottle made a great impression on him, and while he was going to and fro from kitchen to courtyard, to sheepfold, while he stirred up the fire and returned with a bucket of water, his glance went to it incessantly, avid and anxious, while a visible nervous excitement took command of his movements.

Mariutine, curled up on the stone hearth, followed with somewhat dreamy eyes Barbe Zef's comings and goings. The fact of being at home and the warmth of the fire had revived her a bit, but although she cradled Petòti in her arms, from time to time she had the sensation that someone was splashing freezing water down her spine. She was hoarse; she had not yet had the strength to take off her soaked shoes that weighed on her feet like lead. She felt too tired to get up to help Barbe Zef.

He, to be sure, did not look at her, did not call her, did not ask her to do anything, as though he were not even aware of her presence. He had dragged the table closer to the fireplace and had put down two plates and the only soup bowl. Now, dark of face and mumbling to himself, he got ready to uncork the bottle.

That bottle was so tightly sealed that he had to go to a lot of trouble pulling and tugging to uncork it. While he was doing so he muttered ever more suspiciously through his clenched teeth. His hands shook; he squinted his injured eye so tightly that he looked one-eyed. As God willed it, the cork came out. At that, almost pushing his nose into the bottle, the man took a good long whiff of its scent.

'Holy cow! . . . Grappa!' he exclaimed as though a block of stone had been lifted from his chest. 'I was afraid that that freak had played some trick on me.'

And with that he lifted the bottle to his mouth and gulped down a long draught. Then, having taken his place at the table opposite the fireplace, he drew the provisions near him and, resuming his habitual taciturnity, without further delay he began to drink and eat. For a short while nothing was heard except the croc-croc of his jaws and Petòti's, for the dog too, unexpectedly abandoning Mariutine's lap, had thrown himself furiously on the food.

Gradually Mariutine had taken off her shoes. She had extended her soaked feet toward the fire, and, leaning her head against the edge of the fireplace, she had closed her eyes. She was so exhausted that it seemed to her she had no need of food. She even felt a distaste for it. It even provoked a revulsion. All she needed was just sleep and rest. But gripped by a feverish torpor, she was unable either to wake up or to fall asleep. She saw the table, the little mountaineer's lantern diffusing its pink glow all around, Barbe Zef's bent shoulders and earth-colored jacket, Petòti's tail. She heard the crackle and groan of the green wood in the fireplace. The acrid odor of the sheep-fold hurt her nostrils. But other images, sounds, and odors overwhelmed these and alternated strangely with reality.

Now it was the sinister red face of the devil, now the long beard of the old jester, now the dear and gentle face of Ursule and her boyish head with those lovely dark ringlets that danced before her drowsy eyes, and all at once there came to her ear the sharp, penetrating sound of someone blowing his nose like the blare of a hunting horn, or the long notes of the accordion that were lost little by little in the snowy night.

Was she dreaming or was she awake? . . . Was she in her hut or in the farmstead of Compare Àgnul? . . . Her head drooped down onto her chest. She was truly about to fall asleep.

And just then:

'What did the hunchback say to you?' asked Barbe Zef.

Mariutine opened her eyes wide, took a quick deep breath, and sat up straight. She looked at Barbe Zef, but he was not looking at her. Bent over his plate until he was almost touching it, his face pale and his expression dull, he was chewing very very slowly, like a ruminant beast at the trough. Nevertheless he had spoken: she was quite awake.

'He was telling me . . . ' she murmured hesitating, but unable to lie, 'he was telling me . . . that I ought to get a job as a maid in town.'

There was a long pause.

'And you, what did you tell him?'

'I answered that I have to take care of you and my sister and that I prefer to stay at our own home,' Mariutine said in a rush, and her eyes once more rested, worried and uneasy, on Barbe Zef. What if he were in favor of Compare Guerrino's idea and would decide to send her away? . . . One mouth less to feed!

'Good girl!' he exclaimed instead, cheerfully, thumping his fist on the table and for the first time raising his eyes to look at her. '*Good girl!* I've always known, I have, that you're a good girl. You could also have answered him, that dog, that so long as there's Barbe Zef alive, you've no need to seek a mouthful of polenta in anyone else's house, not today and not ever. Come here. Haven't you eaten yet? Why do you stay back there?'

'I'm cold . . . ' murmured the girl, getting up with difficulty to take a seat on the bench next to him. 'And I don't feel like eating.'

'Then drink and be merry,' Barbe Zef said forcefully. 'And you'll see, the coldness will pass.' He put an arm around her shoulders and with his right hand he held out the bottle to her, almost upside down so that she could drink from it.

Mariutine tilted back her head a bit, and a long gulp of the liquid, burning like fire, flowed down her throat.

'Oho, blondie, hold on there!' laughed Barbe Zef, brusquely drawing back the bottle. 'You're getting to like it, eh? . . . First nothing, then too much. But Barbe Zef likes to be fair. We'll take turns. It's my turn now!'

Without releasing the girl's shoulders, he drank again, and then he held out the bottle once more. He offered it to her holding it high up so that she would have to stretch her neck to reach it. Then, when the red fleshy mouth was just about to get there, for a prank he shifted his hand this way and that. Repeatedly, Mariutine, her lips pursed to catch the bottle in its flight, saw it elude her. Finally she managed to intercept it and held it for a moment, but Barbe Zef, laughing like a madman, lunged to repossess it, and she too was laughing in convulsive outbursts, seized by uncontrollable hilarity.

'My turn!'

'Mine!'

Pushing and pulling, first one way then another, all in the game, from the half-empty bottle, a goodly amount poured out to flood her face and neck. Then Barbe Zef's mood abruptly changed. That the grappa had been spilled, that it had been squandered, evidently vexed him, and while he turned the bottle this way and that way as though to measure how much of its contents remained, his face had become grim and surly, while the scar of his injured eye trembled visibly with a nervous twitch.

'The hunchback likes you,' he declared suddenly thumping the bottle on the table with scorn. 'What do you think! . . . That that dog there, who got rich squeezing people he lent money to, sucking the blood of poor folks, profiteering on everybody else's labor, has suddenly become so generous as to make presents of all this stuff just so, without a purpose? Ah, ah, ah! . . . That fellow, you understand, gives not even a drop of water to a dying man unless there's something in it for him. But he's a ladies' man and a libertine. The hunchback's got a protrusion in front as well as one behind. Ugly and old as he is, he hasn't yet let up. He has a house in Belluno . . . I even know where. . . . And he finds his profit there too: he looks out for himself first, and he lets the others have what's left over. That fellow has had more women than he has hairs on his head. All the *fantatis* who took jobs in his mother's household, then all those in the homes of his relatives, and still others, many, many others. He likes you, take it from me. He's got his eye on you. And he expects me to play the pimp.'

Although Mariutine noticed Barbe Zef's irritated tone, she was unable to follow all the twists and turns in the thread of his long discourse and she didn't really understand the reason for his rage. From early childhood she was used to his spontaneous talkativeness, to his arguments, his bragging, and the sudden sentimentality when he was drunk. That evening, if he was not all the way there yet, he did not miss by much. If the things he was saying could seem normal, not so were the gestures with which he accompanied them: the stammers, the wide-eyed stare, the twist of his neck. His face was already so congested as to appear swollen. He absolutely had to be stopped from drinking a single drop more.

Why ever was he so angry with Compare Guerrino? . . . Compare Guerrino had been very kind and generous to them, but then the whole Àgnul family had been good and cordial. An evening like the one they had just spent, who knew when such a time would come again.

Although she had not drunk much, Mariutine's fasting and her tremendous weariness had been enough to transform her depression into a happy optimism, a light-headed carefreeness the likes of which she had never before experienced. In that cabin lost in the middle of the snow, in front of the dying fire, far from everybody else, ignored by all, alone with that half-drunken man, she felt her heart so merry and light that if she had not been afraid to annoy Barbe Zef, she would have begun to croon a little song.

Barbe Zef, on the other hand, with his head between his hands, lost in dark broodings, stared into space, and the portion of his freckled visage around the scar seemed to be laughing, although the rest of his face remained sullen, motionless, and almost lugubrious.

'I tell you,' he resumed in a prophesying tone, pointing his index finger at Mariutine, 'I tell you that this past night, while I was sleeping, *that one* came sneaking into the barn. You don't believe it? . . . I tell you it's true. I saw and heard it. Ah, ah, was he ever comical! He was in his underwear with a hat on his head. He had two humps, one in front and one behind, and his legs looked like the legs of a compass. I knew he was there; but I pretended to snore, whereupon he began to whisper in my ear. And he was saying "*Compare* . . . *Compare* . . . Old friend . . . Old friend. . . . "'

Just what Compare Guerrino had actually said to him, or what Barbe Zef supposed he had heard, Mariutine was not in time to grasp, for, brusquely cutting short his speech, Barbe Zef reached out his arm across the table to get hold of the grappa again.

'No, Barbe, no!' Mariutine exclaimed quickly, and with her right hand she grasped the man's arm in midair and held on to it, while with the other she anticipated him by taking hold of the bottle and gaining possession of it.

Barbe Zef remained staring at the girl for an instant as though dumbfounded by such effrontery. Then, without uttering a word, he raised high his free hand and smacked her full in the face with a slap so hard and brutal that she screamed.

'Barbe Zef!' she exclaimed with tears in her eyes. But she did not relax her grip. On the contrary, with a bound she slid off the bench and moved to the other side of the room. She leapt up onto the raised stone hearth of the fireplace, turned, and put the table between herself and the man.

'Be reasonable, Barbe Zef,' she pleaded from the far side of her makeshift bulwark. 'Don't drink any more tonight. Let me take care of the grappa. I promise to give it back to you tomorrow. But not tonight!'

In silence he continued to stare at her, unmoving, with the one cold and wicked eye. And Mariutine stared back uneasily at him. And neither of the two, one on this side and the other on that side of the wobbly old table, budged.

But unexpectedly she coughed, and this was enough to make the man fling himself toward her to grab hold of her.

Although dazed by the alcohol, he sprang here and there like a chamois. He staggered and stumbled, but he recovered immediately, mumbling between his teeth so unclearly that she could not tell whether he were cursing or laughing.

And she eluded him deftly, the way a mouse runs away from a cat. Holding one hand to her reddened and throbbing cheek, she tightly clenched the bottle of grappa in the other.

Childlike, she had already forgiven Barbe Zef his slap in the face, and she pretended to be more afraid of him than she actually was; as a matter of fact that pursuit and her own adroitness in not getting caught filled her with pleasure and hilarity as though it were all a game. Youthful pride in not getting caught excited her. How many times, in the farmyards of the homesteads where once she used to pass through with her mother and Rosùte, had she run and played that way, 'ai quattro canti,' the game of four corners, without any of the boys her own age succeeding in catching her!

The kitchen was so narrow that their scuffle was concentrated between the fireplace and the table. Like a barricade, the table protected and separated the grappa and Mariutine from Barbe Zef's assaults, and that was the advantage she could not afford to lose.

In the fireplace the last glowing embers were burning

feebly, and only the mountaineer's lantern, its glass murky and smoked, cast out a little circle of light. Petòti, not knowing what was going on, ran here and there, now at Barbe Zef's heels and now at Mariutine's, and his crazy spurts of barking expressed at one and the same time both supreme pleasure and perplexity.

All at once, perhaps because of a false step, perhaps because of a momentary distraction, Mariutine is about to lose her advantage. The hands and heavy breath of Barbe Zef are upon her.

'Ah! . . . '

Instead of running around the table, she springs to stand upon it, and with a leap she jumps down on the other side, but Petòti, completely losing his head, catches her by the skirt, and table, lantern, girl, and bottle tumble down to the ground all in one heap.

There was heard the shattering of broken glass, the crackle of old wood splintering, the furious barking of Petòti—then, utter darkness and silence.

Thus several moments passed. Then, from that heap of broken pieces, subdued sobs issued forth, and between the sobs, a worried voice began to plead, 'Forgive me, Barbe Zef. I didn't do it on purpose, Barbe Zef. I fell; I didn't mean to break the bottle, Barbe Zef.'

There was no reply.

Falling, Mariutine had cut herself on a piece of glass, and blood trickled from her wrist, but she did not seem to care about that, nor did she feel her pain, so completely was she gripped by remorse and fear. The fact that she had smashed the bottle of grappa seemed to her childlike mind an enormous, unpardonable sin.

'*He* surely believes that I threw it to the ground on purpose so as not to give it back to him, out of stubbornness,' she thought, and her sobs became stronger and more grief stricken.

She did not dare get up and walk around, for fear of

colliding in the darkness against Barbe Zef, whose deep silence worried her, and she stayed there on the ground crying, trying vainly, through her tears, to see through the dark and to understand at least where *he* was, and what he was doing. But she could discern absolutely nothing, except, from moment to moment, Petòti's eyes, brilliant as two electric bulbs, in the farthest corner of the kitchen. Petòti too stayed stock still and was afraid.

Feeling with her hand the floor and the walls around herself, Mariutine had been able to discover exactly where she had fallen. Some empty sacks, damp and redolent of mold, piled up in that corner for some time, had prevented her from cracking her head against the stone hearth of the fireplace. She was without shoes, and she was cold. Her slight intoxication had wholly evaporated.

'Barbe Zef!'

No sign at all from him; but his presence was as palpable as that of a huge beast—his presence, his breath, his anger, his life. All that *existed;* it was there; and it seemed that the silence was full of it, that it vibrated only from that and for that.

'Barbe Zef, forgive me!' Mariutine repeated imploringly. 'I swear to you that I didn't do it on purpose. I beg your pardon on bended knees, Barbe Zef! . . . '

And no one replied. But perhaps he was walking along the wall, perhaps he was moving on all fours, groping his way, in the dark? . . .

'Where are you, Barbe Zef? Why don't you speak?' asked Mariutine in agony, raising herself up to a sitting position, straining her ears.

And at that two rough hands grabbed her by the thighs, a craving mouth sought her breasts, and Barbe Zef threw himself on her and violently took her.

*

It was nighttime when Mariutine regained consciousness and realized what had happened. Measureless time had elapsed between the last moment, which she remembered with horrible clarity, and this moment of her reawakening. Had it been minutes? Had it been hours? . . . She had been thrown outside of her very life. In that time she had not thought, she had not suffered; she had remained there as though dead. Now the physical pain and even worse the dry heat of fever and a burning thirst recalled her to reality. And reality was that male body sprawled with all its weight on top of her body, those disheveled clothes, that mouth that blew its breath in her face. The man was sleeping. After intercourse, drunkenness had completely prostrated him.

Mariutine suddenly regained full awareness, with a loathing so profound that for several moments she continued to lie beneath him with wide-open eyes, frozen, incapable of the least little voluntary act. She felt entangled in one of those silences where it seems that nothing more can happen; where life, death, joy, and grief seem abolished forever—a silence unlike any other; definitive and final.

Petòti came to lick her hands.

Then little by little, bit by bit, trembling in all her limbs, with infinite precautions she detached from herself one at a time those arms that were still holding her, those feet in their heavy shoes that were bruising her calves, that bald head that was crushing her shoulder. Bit by bit, stretching and squirming with imperceptible movements—almost crawling down into the ground—she succeeded in slipping away from underneath the man, and in putting some distance between herself and him. What burning thirst! How she ached in all her bones! . . .

Water was over there, in the bucket, in the other corner of the kitchen. She went over and drank a great gulp of it, feeling the frost and the smell of earth. Her forehead burned. She had pains and a crick in her neck, and the sense that her entire body was bruised and torn. She sat on the stone hearth of the fireplace, bent way over, with her head touching her knees, utterly exhausted, as though she were about to faint. To faint or to die? . . . Ah, it would be better to die, to stop feeling pain, to stop toiling, to stop knowing! To rest for all eternity, like her poor mamma! . . .

He was sleeping, his snoring like a death's rattle. The shameless abandon of that body covered with earth-colored rags that could have been mistaken for earth itself had some quality of both the grotesque and the mournful. Now he was sleeping. He might go on sleeping for hours and hours perhaps. He was known to have slept for an entire day after having gotten drunk. But what of the next day? And the day after that? . . .

From the little window there entered a glimmer of pallid light. Was it still night, or was dawn near?

Yes, it was dawn. The sheep were bleating. Petòti was barking and scratching at the door to be let out. Life was picking up again: life with its needs, its instincts, its rights, its harsh necessities. And above all the harsh and stinging bite of hunger and cold. . . .

There was almost a whole loaf of bread on the table, and she grasped it even before her will and thought told her to take it. She grasped it and brought it to her mouth without breaking off a piece, biting at it voraciously, swallowing large chunks without chewing, almost without drawing breath. She ate and she cried. Tears flowed down her cheeks, and their salty taste mixed with the taste of the bread.

Then, moved by the same dominating instinct, she crossed the kitchen like a somnambulist, went to the shed where the firewood was kept, and loaded a bundle on her shoulders. She came back in great haste and lit the fire.

And tomorrow? . . . And the day after? . . .

✳

And the next day the sun rose as always bit by bit in the heavens, it set behind the high peaks that took on an overall pinkish hue. The flock went out to go to the stream, and it returned to the sheepfold. Petòti ate, barked, slept. The owls of Bosco Tagliato sent forth their lugubrious hoots through the air, and then they were silent. Darkness fell on the mountain, with nothing, absolutely nothing, arising to show or remind that something abnormal had occurred.

That same night, Mariutine had carried the blankets and Barbe Zef's rags into the hen coop, and when he awoke from his heavy drunken sleep, he had done his best to make up his pallet, without raising any objections.

The following nights she waited before going to bed until she was certain that he was asleep, and only then did she enter her cubbyhole cautiously, and slowly very slowly, on tiptoe, scarcely breathing, in order not to remind the one who was stretched out on the other side of the thin wall of her existence, she piled up against the door as many heavy objects as she found near at hand.

She did not undress. With a blanket over her, with her shoes on her feet, she stretched out on the high, creaking bed, and for hours at a time, shivering with cold and fear, she was unable to close her eyes.

But nothing happened. The longest nights, the shortest days, passed calmly and without any change.

She did not sing any more, but she attended to her chores with a busyness rendered the more intense by her need to escape 'that thought.' *He* came and went as usual from the cabin to the woods to the coal pile. He could be heard hammering under the shed, or whistling beside the fire carving miniature wooden rakes, buckets, ponies, bowls, and spoons. He had no longer gone down to town. He was content with a bowl of *jote* and a gulp of water. His dark and dull face revealed no trace of a reaction to any sort of memory. He had drunk a bit too much and he had slept through an entire day. Waking, he had resumed his customary life: that was all.

If there was any slight shade of difference, it was no more than a greater irritability on his part. He now opened his mouth to speak to her scarcely two or three times a day, and only when forced to do so. At such times his eyes avoided meeting Mariutine's. That was all.

She finally felt reassured.

✳

The sky's clarity and the depth of the snow cover that under the piercing cold was hardening into ice announced a winter of exceptional severity. January twenty-seventh! . . . Two weeks from the day on which they had taken Rosùte to the hospital in Forni, met Compare Àgnul at the Little White Horse Inn, and spent the night at the dairy farm where the three girls lived. . . . How far away all that seemed! Two weeks, and Mariutine had not yet gone down the mountain to see her sister. She had, it could be said, hardly thought any further of her, so much had grief and shock for her own person preempted her attention.

The mysterious thread that binds two creatures who love each other and makes them, when close, understand each other with a single, wordless glance, and even when far apart enables one to feel the thought and virtually hear the voice of the other, that mysterious thread, which solitude and misfortune had tightened all the more strongly between her and Rosùte, had been momentarily broken. Rosùte! . . . Ah, Mariutine had not forgotten, no. But darkness had descended upon her, and in those shadows the image of her sister, the only one who would perhaps have been able to give her some comfort, had foundered and been engulfed.

Now it returned. Now in her heart she felt her dear little Rosùte call to her and reproach her: 'Why, why, Mariutine, did you desert me like that?' And she seemed to see her everywhere: along the stream; following the sheep; asleep there beside her in bed; sitting in the sunshine on the threshold of the cabin with her unruly tuft of hair and her bandaged leg as she had so often been only recently.

Who knows with what impatience, but also with what trust Rosùte had waited for them there at the hospital the previous Sunday. . . . With what eyes she had seen the relatives of the other sick children fill the wards, entertaining them while she remained all by herself without anyone, anyone at all, at her bedside! And yet until nighttime she had no doubt kept on waiting, believing, *being certain!* . . . And the hours passed, and one by one the visitors went away. In the rooms the lights were turned on, supper was distributed, the nun entered to conduct evening prayers. . . . Poor little Rosùte! . . . Ah, perhaps she had not complained, she had not let anyone see her cry, but across the distance Mariutine felt with keen pain the suffering of that disappointed little heart.

'Why, why, Mariutine, did you desert me like that?' The sorrowful voice of her little sister called her now with such insistence that she was shaken to the depths of her soul. It was absolutely necessary to go down to Forni the next Sunday. But to go down, she absolutely needed Barbe Zef. A woman alone, no matter how strong and how experienced in mountain skills, could not, with a snow of that sort, risk the double trek across the valley.

She needed Barbe Zef. And since he did not open his mouth, either about this nor about anything else, to need him meant to confront him, talk to him, and come to some agreement. It meant, in a word, to break the fragile barrier of silence between them, and break it to make a request that maybe would displease him. During all that time he had never referred to Rosùte or to her malady, far less to the desire of seeing her again.

Mariutine felt deeply reluctant to ask a favor of Barbe Zef, but her eagerness to see her sister again overcame all other considerations. Finally, after having hesitated for a long time, postponing and repeating in her mind an infinite number of times what she ought to say to him, and just how, she decided with pounding heart to confront Barbe Zef. But he was gone. In vain she sought him under the shed, in the woods, at the coal pile, in all the places he was accustomed to be and to go to.

Barbe Zef had vanished. And vanished too was the old military overcoat, legacy of the soldiers from wartime, that he used to put on sometimes during great cold spells, and the good shoes, which he laced on only when he went down to town. It was a Thursday; the weather was perfect. He had evidently left quite early in the morning, and without saying anything, without telling her: something that since Catine's death had never before happened.

Lunchtime, and suppertime, and those interminable hours of the long winter evening, passed one by one, and there was nothing new. From time to time Mariutine would open the door of the hut part-way and send Petòti out.

'Listen, Petòti, listen! Is your master coming? . . . '

It was already dark. She was seized with worry. The mountain was so treacherous that even the most expert mountaineers had reason to fear it. Might something bad have happened to Barbe Zef? Despite everything, he was the only human being who prevented her and her sister from feeling completely alone and abandoned in the world; he had retrieved and sheltered them instead of leaving them to go begging. From their earliest recollections he was part of their lives. Despite everything, Barbe Zef was family and home. She owed him gratitude and was still naively fond of him.

'Listen, Petòti, listen! . . . '

But Petòti, quite unwilling to go out into that frozen waste, would hastily come back inside with his tail down low, without giving any sign that he had heard anything. Sometimes the dog had a way of looking with a half-shut eye and a doltish expression that made him strangely resemble his master.

Although the fire was lit and constantly kept going from morning on, the cold was such that the water in the bucket had crusted with ice.

She waited and waited. Finally Mariutine persuaded herself that it was absurd to think that at that time of night and with that outdoor temperature Barbe Zef was on his way back to the hut. No, he would be sleeping over at some farm or inn at the foot of the mountain, and waiting up for him during the night was totally useless.

Finally she decided to go to bed. If at least Barbe Zef, going down to Forni, had gone to see Rosùte! . . . Could he possibly not have thought of it? . . . But at any rate this mysterious journey of his, such a short time before Sunday, certainly made it all the more difficult to ask him for another trip soon to see the child and get him to grant her wish.

Despite the certainty that by now he would not be returning that night, Mariutine remained awake for a long while, listening. The silence was so absolute that she heard her heart beating, and she would have heard the least breath. Only from time to time came the horrid hoot of the owls of Bosco Tagliato. . . .

She was not afraid. In her place, any other girl deserted throughout a long night in a cottage lost on a mountainside would have wept and quaked. But life had been so harsh for her, and had brought experiences so different from those of the majority of children her own age, that the most peculiar circumstances, discomforts, privations, and dangers of every kind found her not unaware or agitated as a child might have been, but inured and almost resigned to suffering like an old woman.

Time passed. She had finally dozed off when the creak of the door and the noise of a footstep woke her suddenly. Petòti had not barked. A whiff of cold air blew across her face. She pulled herself to a sitting position on the bed with her heart thudding.

With his huge overcoat on his shoulders and the lit lantern in hand, Barbe Zef was already in the room. All this was so fast and unexpected that Mariutine could not hold back a cry. But instantly she felt she had to conceal her fear and prevent the other one from recognizing it.

'Ah, it's you,' she stammered, trying to speak in a calm voice. 'It's you, Barbe Zef. Now I'm getting up to light the fire and warm up some soup for you.'

'Never mind,' said the man, taking off his overcoat. He threw it frozen stiff in a corner on the ground and put the little lantern on the lid of the chest.

'A bit of hot soup will do you good. Now I'm getting up,' she urged eagerly, without taking her eyes from him, but without moving, locked into that position and gesture. 'Did you stop at Forni? Did you see Rosùte? How come you went down without telling me?' She spoke nervously, without waiting for an answer, trembling lest silence should fall between them.

'I'm sleepy,' he announced with a long yawn, and moved two uncertain steps toward her.

Mariutine had gone to bed completely dressed and with a rapid movement she got up from the bed. The awareness and the fear of danger were upon her, but she also hoped to sidetrack him, to divert him from what he was thinking.

'First you eat and then you sleep, Barbe Zef,' she said firmly, and in saying so she trembled all over. 'Come, come into the kitchen, for there must still be some embers there, and in two minutes I'll light the fire. In the meantime tell me. Did you sell coal? Did you meet anybody you know? Did you go to visit the *frute?*'

And while uttering these words almost without reckoning their significance, trying to distract him, bit by bit she was sidling away from the narrow aisle between the bed and the wall, edging her way carefully, watchful of his movements, spying out the moment when she could slip away unobserved or jump over him with an unexpected leap.

But Barbe Zef was completely blocking the passage with his body and instead of retreating or shifting his position to leave her way clear, he advanced toward her, engulfing himself in complicated explanations.

'The *frute*? . . . No, I haven't seen the *frute*. And who remembers the *frute*. Barbe Zef has no *frute*. Barbe Zef has coal. I stayed at Àgnul's. Ursule has gotten an engagement ring. Can you guess from whom? From the lame fellow, the blond one who played the accordion; you remember? To each his own. The wedding's to be at San Martino, and we're invited. Ah, ah! Your suitor isn't losing sight of you. He's patient, the hunchback! . . . But you, what are you doing? Why are you trying to get away? I don't need to eat. Stay here and let's talk a bit. It's so long since we've had a talk between us.'

With a shudder, Mariutine understood that he was not completely drunk. The unaccustomed talkativeness was still too sensible and coherent to emanate from total debasement. It was rather a so-called 'cheeriness,' that degree of semi-intoxication that alters the exterior of a personality without affecting it deeply, and the man had a simpering smile on his face, but in the half-shut eye was a fleeting reflection of a sly instinctual determination.

It was too late to elude him by surprise. Had he been completely drunk, Mariutine could perhaps have hoped to escape him with shrewdness, or to free herself by flight, or with a push could have sent him tumbling to the ground. But this way, it was vain to delude herself that she could hoodwink him or defend herself against him. The man was in full possession of himself.

Watching him, she understood all this perfectly, and all at once she realized that she was lost. Alone on the mountain with him. To scream, or to run away? Who would have heard her? Who would have come to her rescue? . . . Where was she to go? Where, where, where would she find sanctuary and pity?

Now he had come closer. He put his rough hands on her shoulders almost in a crude caress, he touched her breast, and he gave her little pats on the arms and neck as he would have done to sooth a filly. Helplessness, despair, a deathly inertia—the sense of the futility of every act or word—overpowered the young girl.

Instead of trying to edge further along the side of the bed toward the door, little by little, feebly trying to elude him while he pressed forward, she was backing against the wall . . . until she leaned against it, livid, without tears, her hands hiding her face.

PART FOUR

*I*n the days that followed she seemed to have accepted that too from fate, even as she had earlier accepted all the rest. But she had accepted poverty, solitude, and harsh toil with innocent laughing eyes. She had accepted them singing. 'This,' had suddenly molded her face into hard, sunken lines. In a few days it had aged her by many years.

She had never resembled her mother. Now, despite her blond hair and fair skin, in her expression devoid of animating light she did resemble her.

By now the man went to bed with her at night, and he took her whenever he wanted to, the same way as he ate or slept. He took her without even remembering it afterwards, or—perhaps—feeling intermittently a confused sense of shame and almost of rancor which, when lust had abated, drove him to avoid her rather than seek her out. The evening of his return from Forni, he must have brought some grappa with him and hidden it, perhaps even buried it underground, to drink it unseen, for often his glance had that ambiguous wink and his movements that eager excitement, which in him were the sure sign of alcohol.

Mariutine would notice, but by this time she had given up watching him. Indifference and the deepest apathy filled her heart. Between them an opaque silence hung heavily, and their contacts with each other were marked by fatalism and sadness.

Another Sunday had passed without anyone's going down to Forni to see Rosùte. Barbe Zef seemed completely to have forgotten the little girl, as if she were dead, and not just since yesterday, but for years. Mariutine thought of her every day and every moment of the day. In the mortal indifference that had fallen to crush her heart, that was still the one live spark. And yet an undefinable feeling of shame, grief, and searing humiliation made it impossible for her to meet Rosùte's eyes. They knew each other so well, the sisters. Each one knew how to read the other's mind so accurately that they could not keep secrets from each other, and it seemed to Mariutine that Rosùte, at the very first glimpse of her, would have surely screamed aloud.

She tried in vain to gain control of herself, to be reasonable. In vain she tried to reassure herself that since nothing was outwardly altered about her appearance, Rosùte was too young and innocent to be able, even if she tried to guess, to come close to the truth of the matter. And so as the days passed, her reluctance to go to see her sister, instead of becoming less, grew, and with it also grew her many-layered suffering.

Suffering that was not exclusively of the spirit. The weary features, the pallor of her face, and the bitter creases around her mouth did not reflect only the profound changes which, without being able to define them, she felt in herself—the destruction of everything that could mean happiness, hope, and love. There was also a strange physical malaise that exhausted her in every fiber of her being.

The ways of the animals they kept had taught her quite early many of the facts of life. But this sickness that seemed to corrode the roots of her soul and her body, was it possible that it was already—that it *could* be—in such a brief period after her first intercourse with that man, the sign of maternity? A mother, she! . . . A blush suffused her temples and forehead at that suspicion. Her heart beat in her throat. Was it truly possible? And to be alone, completely alone, without any human being in whom to confide or from whom to ask advice and compassion! . . .

Cunningly from day to day Barbe Zef avoided more and more coming face to face with her. He barely concealed his irritation if she offered to help him with some task. Whether it was cowardice or embarrassment on his part, she did not exist for him except when, by night, without seeing her face, without hearing her sobs, the way the male dog takes the bitch, he would take her, then let her go, and fall asleep.

She felt so sick, so humiliated and alone, that at times she believed she was going crazy. On certain days that seemed never-ending, grey, monotonous, and all alike, the need to break the atrocious silence and communicate with some living being drove her to talk with the sheep or with Petòti. Or else she fled running from the hut and reached Bosco Tagliato, where she entered into the cut-over area of stumps. There she would fling herself upon the ground between one stump and another, with her face against the earth. Thus she remained for a long time, motionless, without feeling the cold, without crying, almost without thinking. . . . Ah, if the chill of death would only cut her down, and put her to sleep forever! . . .

Instead, bit by bit, her discomfort and agitation abated. A sense of peaceful resignation descended on her heart. She would rouse herself and sit up. She would look about her. . . . Why did she seek out that place? She herself did not know. Her feet carried her there without her even noticing where she was going. Perhaps not for herself alone, but for everyone, for everyone, life was like this: a mutilated wasteland? . . . Perhaps even in this solitude and mutilation, it was possible, and even necessary, to accept life? . . .

No one had taught her to pray. For her, hope or light could not come down from heaven, but, if at all, from earth. Ah, but not from Pieri. Now, the memory of him doubled her misery. To think of him, now, was by far the most cruel part of what so tormented her.

But another being existed on earth from whom a bit of comfort and the ghost of a smile could still come: Rosùte. . . . To have Rosùte, wasn't that already a gift, a hope, and a reason to go on living? . . . Many people have no one in the world. The blind man whom she had met once by the river had no one, no one in the world, except his old dog. Soon Rosùte would return; one must think of life, not of death.

By a strange contradiction, while Mariutine was so fearfully drawing back from the idea of going down to Forni to visit her little sister in the hospital, the thought of the child's return to the hut in the near future, the thought of having her always close again, seemed like her own salvation. How the miracle would work, she didn't understand clearly, but she was sure that upon Rosùte's return even her terrible predicament would have to change.

It was late. She could hear the barking of Petòti, who, at the edge of the area of stumps yet without daring to enter it, was uneasily summoning her. It was the time of day when wolves come down toward the valleys. Not a voice reached out from the plain, not a sign of the presence of human beings. The summits of Cridola and Tudaio rose up merciless before her eyes. A tragically motionless natural setting, veiled in deadly whiteness, surrounded the area of stumps over which the shadows of evening were rapidly falling. Only from the woods close by, despite the intense cold, slight noises, rustlings, and suppressed whispers announced the presence, or reawakening, of a mysterious nocturnal life.

In a short while the owls would begin to send forth through the air their funereal hooting. . . . It was late. She had to go back. She began to walk. . . .

✳

When she realized that Barbe Zef had furtively gone down from their clearing a second time, a rush of indignation roused her heart. A sack of coal, his good shoes, and his overcoat were missing. He had gone down to Forni.

Ah, she had never hated him, and even now she was incapable of hating him. She had endured everything: the repugnant sexual coupling and cruel solitude; the violence and indifference. But this, this, to steal away like a thief without coming to any agreement with her about the child, to return probably like the last time without having seen Rosùte, without even having remembered her, seemed to her such cruelty and inhuman selfishness, as to stir her entire being into a burst of rebellion.

She was feeling so sick that morning, stunned and exhausted as after a fever. Her lips were parched. Little red blisters which she could not account for had suddenly appeared on the palms of her hands. Other strange symptoms on her body profoundly disturbed her.

At night, she had dreamed that Rosùte, instead of getting better, was getting worse, and they had to amputate her leg. Dreams, that's all they were, deriving from feverish excitement and from an obsessive thought that gnawed at her like a worm. She did not believe in dreams, and yet she had awakened with a start all the same, as if a frozen talon had seized her heart: She had abandoned her baby sister! . . . And that dream left such a strong impression on her, that if Barbe Zef had told her, 'Today I'm going to Forni,' overcoming every shame and every hesitation, she would have gone down with him or at least she would have forced him to swear to her that he would himself go without fail to the hospital to bring back news. Wasn't it necessary, even urgent, to find out by what date Rosùte would be released?

But maybe . . . maybe this time he had done it of his own accord. Was it possible that his heart was dried up to the point of totally abandoning a darling little one who after all belonged to him? Was it possible that he could once more pass by in front of the hospital without raising his eyes to those windows, without knocking at that door, without remembering Rosùte? . . . Why even imagine such inhuman coldness, before being sure of it? Why judge him so harshly?

Her physical discomfort, meanwhile, was increasing, and it returned to demand her entire attention. She took a piece of broken mirror and looked at herself. She saw reflected in it a wasted face and two eyes encircled by deep rings. Even her hair, until then floating and airy like a golden cloud, had become an opaque shade of blond, dry and without luster. And what about those red blisters? . . . Ah, she was sick, more sick than she had thought. But what was wrong with her? What was wrong? . . . What should she do? What should she think?

Suddenly she remembered having gone once with her mother to consult a woman who had a reputation among the mountain people for possessing great wisdom. It was said that she could cure the most stubborn ailments with juices of mountain grass, poultices, and concoctions that she herself put together. She lived in complete solitude in a hut a little higher up Malga Varmost on the southern slope of Tudaio. That time with her mother, the two of them had gone up at the onset of winter, when the shepherds and herdsmen had already abandoned the mountain, and Mariutine remembered little or nothing about the woman. There had remained only the impression that she was an old acquaintance of her mother's. Nothing else.

Should she go there? . . . Should she take advantage of Barbe Zef's absence to run and seek her out? She was a woman, at least, a person like herself, a human being. . . . But years had passed since the day she and her mother had made that journey, and that woman could be dead, or have moved, emigrated to some distant mountainside. To reach Malga Varmost, in those snowy conditions and weak as she was, would take not less than two good hours of walking. She knew the way, but what if she found the woman no longer there?

She felt so ill, physically so distraught and depressed. Doubt continually surfaced that Barbe Zef might return without having seen Rosùte, reinforcing her worry, adding uncertainty to uncertainty. Inertia and the passivity of waiting became more tormenting to bear than any danger. She could not go on living this way.

She made up her mind. She had no money to offer the woman, nor anything else that might be considered of value; and so she took a little mold of ʄuc. She wrapped it in a white napkin, flung her shawl over her shoulders, put on her snowshoes, and set off.

Petòti joyfully took his place at her side, and this time she did not have the heart to order him back. The dog seemed to intuit that the girl needed guidance and encouragement, for he at once began deliberately to go on ahead of her, turning around from time to time to wait for her and look at her. After the first steps, she no longer felt either weariness or cold, and from the dog's gaze she took a certain comfort.

✳

And she walked and walked and walked. . . . Close to Malga Varmost, the terrain became gentler and the solitude less disconsolate. With a sign of relief Mariutine began to encounter the frozen-over broad clearings of pastures, the folds, a lean-to; and much before she expected it, there it was low and dark in the middle of a completely white meadow—the hut.

It had a sad and abandoned appearance, and it would have seemed completely deserted except that on the ground floor, beyond the glass of a tiny window, a rosy glow indicated a lit fire and the presence of human life.

With a nod, Mariutine enjoined Petòti not to bark. She approached the little window holding her breath. She raised herself up on tiptoe and looked into the hut's interior. Through the window with its little panes plastered together with dried dung, she could barely discern two figures, of whom one seemed to be seated on a low little bench, the other kneeling or curled up on the floor beside the fire. She could not discern them well. They looked like two shadows. But if one of them was the woman whom Mariutine had come looking for, she was not alone. The girl felt all her excitement, all her impatience unexpectedly ebb. How could she dare? . . . Not because of the long trek, but only now out of perplexity and shame, now that she had reached her goal, she was losing heart.

For a few moments that seemed an eternity to her, she remained uncertain and shivering outside that closed door, anxiously examining the two unknown figures on the other side of the tiny window. Should she knock or run away? . . . To run away meant to give up on knowing the cause and the facts of her illness, to sink again into her former terrible apprehension. To knock meant to accept the harshest of punishments, to expose her secret there, in front of human eyes, and expose herself to indifference, curiosity, disdain, everything that can wound and insult, but—perhaps too—to know the truth, gain a little peace, and become somewhat less unhappy.

Should she enter, or should she run away?

Petòti decided for her. Slinking away from his mistress, he had sniffed around here and there with a dissembling air. Then, as if he were not up to anything, he stood firmly on his four legs in the very middle of the little courtyard, and with full force, he began to bark. He put his heart and soul into a great bout of barking.

Mariutine scarcely had time to step back a bit. One of the figures from beside the fire got up and moved silently toward the window. With a squeak the little window opened just the barest crack, and in the narrow opening someone's face appeared. It was a woman, more than old, decrepit, her face furrowed with deep wrinkles, with a black kerchief tied beneath her chin. Yet, although many years had gone by, even more than recognizing her, Mariutine *felt* that it was she, that woman she was looking for, the one whom on that remote day her poor mother had consulted.

The woman stared at Mariutine diffidently, and in her wasted face her eyes were black and sharp.

'Who are you?'

'I'm the daughter of Catine from Bosco Tagliato. I was here once before with my mamma.'

'And your mamma, where's she?'

'She's dead. Four months ago.'

'What do you want?' The woman questioned her in a harsh, firm tone that contrasted strangely with her decrepit appearance.

Before answering, Mariutine lifted up to the height of the little window the mold of *çuc* wrapped in the white napkin.

'I brought you this,' she said in a low and trembling voice. 'And I'd like to speak with you, if you'd do me the favor of letting me in.'

Through the grille a hand reached out to grasp the wrapped bundle. The other figure crouched beside the fireplace had not made any movement.

'Are you alone?'

'Alone.'

The woman disappeared, and an instant later a laborious footstep approached the door, the heavy chain was drawn from within, and Mariutine entered.

At first her eyes uneasily searched out the second person whom she had looked in upon from outside, and who now was bound to be present at their conversation.

And she saw, seated on the ground on a piece of old blanket, like tots before they learn how to walk, a strange creature of no particular age, of uncertain gender, with a huge head on narrow shoulders, and wearing a smock of rough dark wool. His hair was gone white as with age, his forehead was wrinkled like that of an old man, but his azure blue eyes were clear and infantile. He held between his hands two or three little stones that had become smooth and almost polished by dint of having been handled so much, and with these he was quietly playing.

The woman resumed her place beside the fire. Mariutine, shivering and upset, remained standing, just inside the threshold. The woman repeated: 'What do you want?'

Wordlessly, the girl nodded toward the creature there on the floor.

A shadow passed over the woman's wrinkled face. Without replying, she took the poker and began to stir up the fire. She prodded it, scattered it, and ransacked among the embers. She beat and beat again on a thick log, making the sparks fly.

'He is simpleminded . . . ' she murmured finally without looking at Mariutine, meanwhile continuing to stare at the embers almost as if addressing herself, or the fire. 'Simpleminded. . . . He doesn't speak or hear. He is spared life's major mistakes and major griefs.'

She had spoken sententiously, but in an extremely low voice and almost with sweetness. Then, resuming her previous harsh tone, she repeated for the third time, 'What do you want?'

Rather than reply, Mariutine silently began to weep.

The woman detached her gaze from the fire and fixed black and penetrating eyes on the young girl. She looked her over in a rapid inspection from head to foot, her pale face, her eyes from which ran down rare, burning tears.

'Have you had relations with men?'

Mariutine assented with a nod, not uttering a word.

The woman rose abruptly and drew near her.

'If you are pregnant,' she said in a cold and cutting voice, 'and if you have come for me to rid you of it, go away right now. There's nothing to be done here. I'm not getting mixed up in this business. Go away.'

'No, for God's sake, don't send me away!' sobbed Mariutine. 'I've come to you to find out, to have advice. I don't know, I don't believe, I am . . . what you are thinking. It's been such a short time. . . . For several days I've felt so sick, I think I have fever, but I don't know what could be wrong with me. I've come such a long way to get to you, don't chase me away! First, look!' And she held out toward the woman her two open palms, pierced by innumerable red blisters.

Shaking her head and muttering between her teeth, the woman reluctantly took first one of Mariutine's hands and then the other between her own hands and inspected them attentively. Then she looked at the inner lids of her eyes and her gums. She asked her some questions in a low voice.

'Yes, no, yes . . . yes . . . ' replied Mariutine. And a strange disconsolate certainty came over her from that hand that was touching hers, from the closeness of that scrutiny, and from the sound of that voice, which yet had nothing in it of encouragement or affection.

'How old are you?'

'Fifteen . . . I had a birthday last month.'

'I can't do anything for you. Whether or not you're pregnant, I don't know, it's too soon to know. But you're sick with the French disease. If you've come to me to know the truth, that's the truth. You wanted some advice? Go right away to the hospital to get yourself seen and cured by a doctor. You've no time to lose.' The woman had pronounced her verdict slowly, almost sounding out the words syllable by syllable, without taking her eyes from the young girl.

'But why . . .' stammered Mariutine. 'Why do you. . . . Can't you do anything for me? Prescribe a remedy for me, some medicine. I know you've cured and healed so many people. I know it. Why don't you want to take care of me?'

'I set broken legs and arms, I do what I can for pneumonia, I treat sciatica and whooping cough. What you've got is beyond my skill. Go see a doctor.'

'I came to you. I have full faith in you, and I don't want to go to doctors.'

The woman shook her head. 'Like your mamma,' she said after a silence.

'How like my mother? . . . What do you mean?'

'I'm saying that she too, like you, didn't want to listen to me. She didn't want to go to the doctors. When she came here the first time, a few years ago, besides having the sickness you've got, she was also pregnant and four months gone. Just as I told you, I told her, 'I don't want to know about the one thing or the other. Get yourself under the care of a doctor.' She told me herself, later on, that she had secretly got rid of the pregnancy, before she came to term. . . . You understand? . . . It was like that three or four times; and each time at the risk of her life. . . . Zef helped her. But the disease, that, she had to keep that; and what with one thing and the other, the last time she was here, death was looking through her eyes. She was still asking me for advice, but what could I advise her, by then? If you had told me today that she was still on this earth, I would have been more astonished than I am at hearing you say that she's dead.'

Mariutine had listened, and she had heard, but she did not seem to have understood. She was not crying any more. With dry and troubled eyes she stared at the woman who was there in front of her. . . . There was chaos in her mind. . . . Her mamma . . . Barbe Zef . . . A whole un-suspected vista, that she knew nothing about . . . The ignorance of childhood broken by tragic bolts of light . . . Details that had escaped her and now came back to her memory, exact and obvious . . . Her mother's silences . . . And her way of withdrawing physically, refusing to give her or Rosùte even a kiss . . . Her constant alarmed vig-ilance, her constant suspicion . . . And her pent-up grief, desperate and hopeless . . . And her pale face, and her being suddenly and prematurely cast into old age and then death . . .

'I could have kept silent,' continued the woman. 'But you're still almost a child and you're alone. . . . In all good conscience I warn you, be sensible; don't do what your mother did!'

Perhaps the silence and the marblelike immobility of the girl, or perhaps something that against her will passed over her face, struck the woman even more than had the tears and the words.

'If you're tired, before getting on your way back, you can stay a while near the fire, and have a rest,' she said in a voice that had grown kind. 'And don't give up. At your age, if you take care of yourself right away, you can be completely cured.'

But by now Mariutine had nothing more to say and nothing more to listen to. Even the look, even the voice of the woman, and the waves of heat of the fire that struck her in the face, hurt her, inflicted pain on her, made her heart bleed. If in the chaos of her mind one thought, one wish prevailed, it was that of leaving, of being beyond that wall, beyond that hedge, beyond any place in the world whatsoever where there were human beings. . . .

Instead of moving closer to the fire, she took a step toward the door.

'You're going? . . . ' asked the woman, without otherwise trying to detain her. 'If you'd like, after you've been to the doctor's, come back. This whole year you'll find me here. Afterwards, no. I'm too old to spend another winter up here . . . alone.' She passed her hand over the whitened head of the creature who had continued to amuse himself by playing with the stones. 'This one is happier than all of us,' she murmured. 'Well . . . be brave!'

'Thank you, and good-bye,' replied Mariutine with great effort. She reached the door, opened it, and followed by the dog she set out running down the mountain.

It was only after sunset that she returned to the hut. Where and how she had wandered all that time, she wouldn't have been able to explain. For hours and hours she had run and walked aimlessly, that's all she knew. She had wandered through the mountains, she had stopped along the stream, she had penetrated deeply into the woods, she had lost her way, had backtracked, had gone astray again. . . . But perhaps she had also cried out, wept, and talked to herself like a madwoman? . . . Had she thought about dying? . . . Had it been fever and fasting that made her feel, as she went running through the woods, that the squirrels grazed her face with their long bushy tails, and that a pack of howling wolves was chasing her toward the stream—but had they really?

She did not know.

Huts, flocks, shepherds, Àgnul's dairy farm, the villa of Donna Emmelina, all had emerged as if by magic from the snow before her eyes; all had vanished. Light as a shadow her mamma had walked for a long time beside her, and suddenly she had abandoned her. Mariutine had remained alone in the vast solitude. . . .

On the mountains something like a pallor descended. From the plain the fog lifted along the banks of the stream and rose up in billows until it reached the vales. At that point by an instinct stronger than her will, the way a lost dog returns to its own kennel, her feet had carried her back to the hut.

When she reached the threshold, she saw that the fire was lit and that Barbe Zef, already back and seated on the usual low bench with his back to the fire, was calmly nibbling at bread and cheese. Two or three hens came and went at his feet plucking the crumbs he let fall. At seeing him, the girl had a violent and instinctive impulse to retreat, but she conquered it and went in. Petòti ran toward the man with joyous wagging of his tail. He raised his head and greeted her jovially.

'Oh, my blondie! Where are you coming from? Did you have a fine walk?'

He was in one of his talkative and facetious moods, his eyes lustrous, the pale scar prominent on his flushed face.

Without answering him, keeping her hands hidden and wrapped in the edges of her shawl like two stumps, she sat down just inside the doorway.

'The postman in Forni gave me something for you,' winked the man. 'Wait, where did I put it? . . . ' And he searched and searched in the deep pockets of his jacket, from which he drew out a picture postcard all black and crumpled, and he folded it. 'He kept it ten days,' he added. 'Here, catch!' and he tossed it to Mariutine.

The small paper rectangle fell into her lap. Tired and indifferent, her eyes rested on it, then they moved away. Then they focused wide open on the address and on the few words that were written in elegant penmanship beneath a seascape. With difficulty she made out: *'Signorina Maria Zef—A greeting from Genoa—Pietro.'*

The postcard dropped from her hand and fell to the floor. She did not bend to retrieve it. She had closed her eyes and leaned her head against the wall.

'I stopped at Forni,' continued Barbe Zef cheerily. 'I sold a sack of coal to the innkeeper at the Little White Horse. I saw the Àgnuls. The old man's dead. They found some twenty rolls of bread hidden in his straw mattress, hard as rocks. He used to snitch them and hide them; he was like the magpies. The Àgnul family wanted me to eat with them. Good people! . . . And the hunchback . . . oh, the hunchback, he accompanied me for a good stretch of the way constantly talking about you. He gave me the address of his place in Belluno, if ever we go out that way for the fair: Via del Sale 34. Guess what he told me? Naturally I didn't pay attention to him; but it's good to know, it's good to know. . . . Listen. But what're you doing? Are you sleeping? . . . '

She reopened her eyes—and they were huge eyes that in her sunken and pallid visage appeared almost black—and she stared at him. An inner shudder shook her all over. ' . . . Did you go to see Rosùte?'

The words came from her mouth without her having intended to speak, unplanned, and so low that they could barely be heard. Yet they resounded in her own ears as if pronounced in a very loud voice, as if they had come from a distant world, and around them fell a great silence.

'Rosùte? . . . ' replied the man. 'No.'

At that she got up from the bench where she had been sitting and without a word, without a cry, she moved closer to him. When she was just behind him she seemed to hesitate, but she straightened up and quick as lightning, grabbing him by the nape of the neck with one hand, she threw herself against him pummeling him with a storm of blows. She struck blindly, violently, on his shoulders, his face, his head, his neck.

Like a trapped animal, he struggled trying to scratch and bite, delivering punches and kicks to ward her off, but hardly had he managed with a wrench to shake himself loose and begin to stand up, when she, with her huge mountaineer's hand accustomed to the scythe and the axe, started in on him again, and she forced him down, again, down, down, violently crushing him, with all the impetus and force of her young body, tripled by extreme passion and suffering. Blurted and vehement phrases, together with Petòti's possessed barking, filled the pauses of the tragic duel.

'My mamma . . . My mamma . . . You caused my mamma's death . . . First you ruined her and then you did her to death . . . Murderer! . . . Coward! . . . Murderer! . . . '

She stopped only when her strength gave out. Her hair had tumbled loose over her shoulders and down over her face. Her skirt was in tatters. Her right hand was bleeding from the man's bite. She let herself fall at the end of the bench from which he had slipped during the struggle. Heedless of his nearness and the danger, indifferent to the possibility that he might take revenge, she collapsed with her head on the table, her face hidden between her arms, and she began to sob despairingly.

The man was perhaps aware of her closeness and her vulnerability, but he did not take advantage of it. He remained there on the ground a little distance from her, who had beaten him up so violently. Curled up on himself, coughing, panting, and spitting, he was also a heap of rags, an old man, he too a poor weak creature, without guile. From time to time he furtively cast a look full of fear on her, and finally he too began to cry quietly. And in this weeping, like a child he repeated his querulous lament: 'Ah, ah, poor Zef! Ah, ah, poor Zef! . . . '

Unable to bear it any longer, Mariutine raised her head, quickly dried her tears, and put her hand on his shoulder. She felt him quiver.

'Enough,' she ordered. 'Tomorrow you'll go to see Rosùte.'

'Yes,' he mumbled.

'You'll tell her that . . . I've been taken ill . . . and that's why till now I haven't been able to go down to Forni. For yourself you'll make up some excuse. The child mustn't suppose that she has been forgotten. Is that clear? Then you'll find out from the doctor there if and when we can bring her back home.'

'Yes,' he repeated.

✳

The endless night had passed without the two exchanging any further words. Mariutine had thrown herself onto her bed completely clothed. The man had remained in the same corner where he had fallen, between the table and the fireplace with the dog beside him, no longer crying, no longer speaking, and without risking the least attempt to change his room and pallet. After a time she heard a regular monotonous noise. He had actually been able to fall asleep! Then, bit by bit, Mariutine too had finally fallen into a heavy torpor.

She wasn't sleeping, no. Her entire being was broken by too much suffering to be able to yield to sleep, but the fleeting excitation had fallen away, and in its place fatigue, fasting, and fever had created an aura of bewildered stupor, almost of unconsciousness, in which the tragic image of her mother and the anguish—the piercing, burning, unbearable anguish—that was born from that image, had clouded over, fading, almost detaching themselves from her. Her trek to Malga Varmost, her wandering through the mountains, and her return to the hut now flowed together in her memory more like a nightmare or a hallucination than like reality.

Words, images, doubts, memories were full of horror and sorrow. Were they in the here and now or far away? Beyond belief, or real? . . . She could not, she could not any longer focus her thoughts upon them for any length of time. Rather there appeared to her unsummoned phantoms, shadows and figures that were comic, cheerful, and crazy: a crowd of masks with weird, ugly faces and flaming eyes, that danced in a circle flinging legs and arms into the air. She saw the hunchback, dressed like a woman, running to her and making her a great bow; and behind him a crowd of young men and girls coming forward laughing and singing:

The sun at sunset is a glory
And the moon splendid above
And the stars they form a crown
And sweethearts are making love.

And she wanted to stop them and join them, to sing, she too wanted to be in their chorus—it was so long, so long ago—since she had sung, or laughed! . . . She opened her mouth to call and moved her hands to make a sign to the singers that they should stop, they should wait for her, but her voice did not want to issue from her throat, and the hands that were waving aloft were hurting her so much, so much; and from them there spurted an uninterrupted flow of drops of blood. . . .

She had wakened suddenly at this vision. Her hands were really paining her, a dull continuous pain. As a matter of fact, it had been that very pain that had wakened her; but her forehead was also on fire, and her pulse raced like a frenzied horse. From head to foot she felt that she was burning up.

Dawn. No more sounds from the kitchen. Where was Barbe Zef? . . . The door of the hut was ajar.

'Petòti!'

No sign of Petòti's presence. There was no one else around. Barbe Zef had taken off without her having heard him, along with the dog.

Mariutine rubbed her hand across her forehead as if to dispel the fog obscuring her memories. . . . Ah, yes, yes; Barbe Zef had gone to Forni to see Rosùte. She herself, the day before, had ordered him to do so. *Ordered* him! The word and the fact brought her back to reality, and consternation overwhelmed her. . . . She, she, the evening before, had attacked and reviled Barbe Zef. She had rained blows on him, thrown him to the ground, and almost trod him underfoot. Only this stood out in her memory, and in such high relief and of such enormity did it seem, that it totally drove from her mind all notion of what had provoked it.

For years, it could be said ever since birth, but especially after her mother's death, her attitude toward Barbe Zef had been that of a suppliant toward the one who doles out charity. An attitude of subjection, of indirect hinting and humility, had become second nature to her. Now, as a dog is able to break loose from the chain to which he is accustomed and can even bite the hand that feeds him, but quickly returns of his own will with lowered tail and full of fear to the collar of slavery, so she bent her shoulders and lowered her head, gripped by terror and remorse over what she had dared.

For twenty-four hours she had been living among monsters and phantoms. It seemed that she was going crazy. What, what in the world, had she done? Clutching her burning temples between her hands, trying to put her thoughts in order, she painstakingly began to call up again one by one the episodes of the previous evening.

She had come into the kitchen . . . Barbe Zef had sat there eating . . . they had exchanged a few words . . . and she had hurled herself upon his back like a wild beast. . . . And he? . . . So far as she could remember, he had only defended himself without excessive brutality. . . . Then he had begun to cry. . . . He had spent the whole night curled up on the floor with the dog. . . . At dawn, obedient to her command, he had gone down to Forni.

But undoubtedly, the night before, when she had rained blows upon his shoulders, alcohol and surprise had induced a state of inebriation and dullness that paralyzed his ability to react and had prevented him from figuring out exactly what was happening. To her broken hints about the past, he had not opposed a word; perhaps he had not understood. And probably he had not understood the reason why she had thus suddenly turned against him, nor even wondered why it had happened. . . .

Tired, soused with alcohol, and struck by surprise. . . . Yes, his passivity and his submissiveness of the night before could be explained up to this point. . . . But what about at dawn when he had left, when the time that had passed and the night's rest must have cleared away even the last traces of alcohol and permitted him to remember. What about then? When he could have easily overcome her while she was still sunk in sleep—to avenge and punish her?—he had instead remained quiet and had obeyed. He had quietly got back on the path toward Forni. . . . But was she really sure that he had gone to Forni? . . . That he had gone to see Rosùte? . . . Couldn't he on the other hand still be there, in the woods or just outside the hut, or hidden in the hut itself? . . .

At this doubt, a terrible uneasiness, a convulsive trepidation took hold of her. The dog had disappeared. That too seemed strange to her and a bad omen.

'Petòti! Petòti!' she went around calling, and pale and disheveled she wandered through the main room to the kitchen, to the sheepfold, to the hen house, keeping her ear tuned for noises. She had shut the door of the hut from within, but a wall that creaked, a bleat, or the flapping of a hen's wings, startled her.

No, not in the house. *He* was not there. The overcoat and the shoes were missing once again. He had left. But to go where? . . .

Mariutine tried to extend her gaze beyond the opaque glass of the little window but she saw nothing. Rocks and snow, snow and rocks. . . . Her agitation was such that she had neglected to do what she did automatically and mechanically every day when she first got up: to light the fire. And even while the chill of the little kitchen penetrated to the bone and intense shivering shook her all over, like an animal in the midsummer heat that runs to the fountain, she continually put her dry mouth to the bucket, and almost plunging her head in, she gulped down long swallows of freezing cold water without being able to quench her thirst.

She would have liked to take a bit of the soft white snow that she saw out there, just a few steps away from the hut, to sink her hands into it, to press a bit of it against her forehead. It seemed to her that that would have given her such peace and such refreshment! . . . But she did not dare open the door again or venture forth outside the hut, for fear of the man.

Ah, if she had been alone in the world, if she had not had Rosùte, she would not have feared for herself! . . . Let Barbe Zef seize her, thrash her to a pulp, hurl her down over the mountain crags. . . . Or else, since he knew how to catch foxes and wolves in a noose, let him one fine morning entrap her too and shoot her dead with a single shot.

If she had not had Rosùte, what value would life have had for her at this point, or what purpose? . . . She would not have stirred a single step to protect herself from death! But there was Rosùte; little Rosùte, motherless Rosùte. . . . To protect, defend, and save her from grief. . . . At least her!

Had he gone to see her? The previous evening he had promised, but that didn't mean anything. When had she ever been able to read something for sure—truth or falsehood—on that obtuse face, that even when he was crying seemed to laugh? If he were still there, in the woods or just outside the hut, from one moment to the next he might reappear right in front of her.

What was she to say to him? . . . Ask him once again, 'Have you been to see Rosùte?' and hear the same reply? Or else say nothing, kneel down before him, beg his pardon, plead with him not to make the little child pay for the blunder that she and she alone had committed? . . . To beg his pardon! . . . When her poor humiliated hands were there to remind her of a foul disease, and to scream out that before her, her mother had been subjected to the same fate, and nothing, nothing had been able to change the course of events, except death. . . . To beg his pardon!

'Yet . . .' she feverishly said to herself, 'yet, I will do it, I will do it . . . I have to think of Rosùte, of her alone. I have to prevent what happened between him and me from having repercussions on that innocent one. I must humiliate myself even more, it is necessary. Yes, for Rosùte I must humiliate myself to the point of asking his forgiveness!'

With evening's fall, nervousness and tension had not yet abandoned her. She tried to gain control of herself, but she was still, as always, afraid. . . . Of what? She didn't know. Of night that was coming on, of silence, of solitude; all those harsh conditions of life that she had always managed to deal with courageously. . . . Fear of the man's return, an obscure sense of the unknown. . . .

In all those hours she had taken no nourishment except a piece of bread and a small leftover portion of ɟuc. The fireplace was without a fire, and the sheep, to whom she had given no thought since the evening before, were crowded together against the door of the sheepfold, bleating, bleating uninterruptedly. Outside, a fierce wind had sprung up. From the corner where habit prompted her to stay, she looked at her hands and listened without hearing to those horrid bleats that pierced her temples. They did not sound like bleats. They sounded like cries . . . cries and moans that were human.

Suddenly, with a profound shock to her soul, in the loud and strident chorus, it seemed she could distinguish and isolate a cry:

'Frutes!' called a voice full of agony. 'Frutes!'

Ah, just as when, as little girls, she and Rosùte had wandered away a bit from their mamma. . . .

'Frutes! . . . Frutes! . . . Frutes! . . . '

Three or four times, among the bleats of the flock and the wheezing of the wind, the anguished cry pierced through space with utmost clarity. Then it was silent.

At that, as if nudged by someone or something that urged her to hurry, she shiveringly leapt to her feet and looked for the oil lamp. She lit it. She fetched an armful of dry grass and threw it to the sheep, then a bundle of firewood, and she stacked it in the fireplace. The fire had hardly begun to blaze up, when two dry knocks were struck upon the door. She heard Petòti's joyous barking. Without any further thought to the living or the dead, she

171

hurried to the door and opened it, and Barbe Zef entered followed by the dog.

✳

And with him came a draft of freezing air that made the lamp and the fire flicker. Enveloped in his overcoat up to his ears, he looked very tired. The journey to and from Forni—if Forni was where he had gone—repeated two days in a row without an interval of rest was enough of an enterprise to do in younger and stronger men than he. Mariutine knew it, and while she furtively cast a worried glance at him, she felt anew the shadow of remorse passing over the spirit, and at the same time she realized two things: that on that day he had not been drinking, and that he was in no mood to talk. Without asking him the question that was burning on her lips and without offering him any other word, she quickly got busy around the fire to heat some soup for him.

He had taken off the overcoat and snowshoes and had sat down in silence on his customary low bench, not this time with his back to the fireplace, but facing it and a bit to the side, so that he could see the fire and the cauldron and observe Mariutine's comings and goings.

His behavior revealed no anger or rancor nor any memory of the least thing that might have displeased him. It was as though infinite time had intervened between the previous day and this one, and yesterday had even been cancelled out of existence. Only, if the girl came near him, the man's shoulders flinched slightly, and the scar of his eye afflicted by a brief tremor betrayed a sort of tense quivering.

She filled a bowl of scalding hot soup to the brim and placed it before him. She felt her fear rapidly vanishing. Nothing of all she had thought, fantasized, and dreaded was coming to pass. If the lame devil of local lore had wanted to spy inside the Zef hut that evening, instead of a bandit thirsty for revenge and a weeping pleading Magdalene whom Mariutine had created in her fantasy, he would have seen a poor bald man, tired and clad in threadbare rags, bent over his bowl of soup, and a young, blond girl, with blue eyes and good manners, who was attentively serving him. Those two creatures, who the day before had so violently clashed, were eating in silence one beside the other in front of a blazing fire.

✳

It was only after having eaten the soup, two huge potatoes roasted in the fire's ashes, and a piece of cheese, that the man decided to talk to her. And drawing from the pocket of his trousers a tiny packet tied with a red string, he placed it carefully at the extreme end of the table.

'Compare Guerrino gave me this for you,' he said.

She was just removing the kettle full of hot water from the fire to carry it to the sink, and without setting it down she turned.

'For me? . . . ' she asked blushing deeply.

'For you,' the man repeated. 'Take it.'

So she put the kettle on the hearthstone of the fireplace, and with uncertain hands she took the packet and opened it. It contained a little box neatly wrapped in tissue paper, and in the box was a necklace of imitation coral, closed by a clasp of gilded metal and placed on a layer of pink cotton.

She stood stock-still as though turned to stone in her amazement. Motionless, holding her breath, with her fingertips, she delicately put the coral necklace to her throat as she would have handled a consecrated wafer, holding it suspended in the air and a bit away from herself, almost fearing to damage it or to dim it with her breath.

Her glance went from the necklace to Barbe Zef with an expression of touching uncertainty and ecstatic admiration. Then, leaving everything aside, kettle water and Barbe Zef, she ran into the next room, found the piece of broken mirror that she used when she combed her hair, and clasping the strand of coral beads around her neck, she stared at her reflection for a long time.

It was the same piece of mirror into which she had looked with such sorrow, but now she no longer saw a wasted face there, two sorrowful eyes, the threadbare poverty of her little jacket. She noticed only that stupendous marvelous thing that she had on herself, those glittering beads around her neck that she had admired so many times at the booths of the country fairs or in the window of the only jeweler in Forni—admired, dreamed about, yearned for, and considered unattainable. She saw it shine around her neck, she twined it in her hair, she brought it close to her cheek, she dangled it full length and let it hang upon her breast. . . . How lovely, how lovely it was!

The beads were small, uneven, and poorly cut. It was certainly not a sumptuous gift. But she had never possessed anything, anything at all to break the bare poverty of her rags, anything to adorn herself with, not even one of those cheap trinkets that the poorest of the girls of her own age had. She asked neither why the hunchback had sent her that present nor whether it was good or bad to accept it. She was fifteen and she was a woman and she felt only an immense, almost incredulous joy.

When she returned to the kitchen, Barbe Zef was in the same place where she had left him, and, what was most unusual, he had lit his pipe. He showed no intention of going to bed. He seemed instead disposed to remain beside the fire for a long while.

Out of bashfulness she had taken the coral beads off her neck. Confused and excited both at once, she held them cupped in her hand, caressing them, brooding over them, almost smiling at those reddish little stones that resembled certain berries she had seen in the springtime on some thorny mountain bush, but more glittering, more shiny, and lovelier; infinitely more lovely.

'Compare Guerrino really said that I can keep them always?'

'Of course!' laughed Barbe Zef.

'They're too lovely to wear every day,' she murmured, and becoming suddenly thoughtful she looked at Barbe Zef, who after supper seemed cheerier and in a better mood. Then the question that was pulsing uninterruptedly in the beating of her heart and that was urging with such an anxious voice for so long, for so long, in her feelings, dared finally to reach her lips and be expressed in timid words.

'Perhaps you went to see Rosùte?'

'Yes,' he replied. 'The *frute* is completely cured. The day after tomorrow she'll be released.'

*

After having answered her this way, with one of those brusque changes of mood that were habitual with him, Barbe Zef did not open his mouth again. Following the smoke of his pipe with his eyes, he sank into his private broodings. Mariutine would have liked to ask him any number of details about his visit to Rosùte: what the little girl had said, and whether she was upset about not having seen them for such a long time, and if she had regained the full use of her little leg, and if she had asked after her . . . but she didn't dare disturb him. . . . Rosùte was coming back . . . she was coming back cured. . . . *He* had not shown any resentment. . . . He seemed to have forgotten the insult he had received.

All this seemed to her a stroke of good luck, a good thing. It was something so wonderful and unexpected that she came near crying. . . . But why, why cry? Surely, when one is used to grief, it is not easy to pass to joy, one is almost afraid to. . . . And she still had her fever, and she still felt so weak. . . .

She had very gently put away the coral beads in their little box, and the box itself in the pocket of her smock, and she had resumed her evening chores; but in washing the dishes and putting the kitchen back in order, she could not restrain herself from occasionally casting a glance full of trepidation toward the pocket that, being distended, remained a bit open, and from lightly touching the little box with her hand as though to pet it.

That night Barbe Zef did not go to bed with her. After having finished his smoke, he went to see to the sheep and the hens; he drew the chain lock of the door, and without explanations, he set up a rudimentary pallet beside the fire, and there he went to sleep. Never, though, could the phrase 'to sleep with one eye only' that customarily refers to dogs have been more aptly applied to a person, for Mariutine heard him at length and repeatedly coughing, sneezing, blowing his nose, clearing his throat, twisting and turning on his pallet, giving in sum all the signs of being much more awake and vigilant than asleep.

*

Next day he did not return for the midday meal. Departing rather early in the morning, he had taken with him some provisions and, giving proof of extraordinary endurance on the eve of yet a third ordeal like the one that awaited him the next day, instead of staying put quietly by the fire, he had gone off wandering through the mountains. Quite truly the mountain was his element. Where others could have found nothing to do and no way to earn a living, he endeavored in a hundred ways, even in the heart of winter, to turn what was available to good use, whether preparing firewood or setting traps for this or that wild animal, and even fishing among the stones of the stream for certain large shrimp that would make up an appetizing dish.

Mariutine too, despite the discomfort that never left her, that day had given herself up obstinately to her work. She was doing laundry, dusting and cleaning, putting the hut and its wretched furnishings back in order from top to bottom in anticipation of her little sister's return. Next day, next day they would be going to bring her home!

'I'll put on the coral beads . . . ' she thought. And while to give up even a small part of them would be like giving away a part of her very self, she had decided to make Rosùte a present of half of them so that she too would have a little necklace.

When at dusk Barbe Zef returned, she was cutting out a little skirt for her sister from an old garment of Catine's. The task was not easy with this fabric all tattered and patched, but with great patience she was hoping to succeed.

Barbe Zef cast a glance at her. 'For whom are you working?'

'For Rosùte.'

'You'd do well to put your stuff more or less in order too, and get your bundle ready,' he said.

Mariutine was holding the shears in her hand and she let them fall to the ground. 'Why? . . . ' she murmured, violently blanching.

'Because, if you're lucky, tomorrow evening you won't be coming back up here,' replied the man calmly. 'Compare Guerrino promised to have you hired as a servant in the household of a respectable family in Belluno, and tomorrow when there's a fair, he has offered to have you make the trip in a barouche with him. He'll be waiting for us early in the morning at the inn, the Little White Horse.'

'And . . . Rosùte?'

'Rosùte? . . . I'll worry about Rosùte. If she can't manage to walk from Forni to here, I'll carry her. But I think she's up to doing it. Now she skips around even better than before.'

'But Rosùte without me, here . . .' stammered Mariutine.

The man observed her with diffidence, and having moved a few step away from her, he took the poker and set about stirring up the fire with a glowering face, without letting his eyes leave her. 'The *frute* is grown up enough to look after herself. And then I'm here,' he said. 'I've supported three of you here for almost ten years,' he added slowly. 'It's only fair that now you too should start earning some money.'

*

After having prepared supper, she went into her bedroom and began to pull out her belongings. Her wardrobe consisted of no more than another jacket and another skirt in every respect similar to the ones she was wearing and just barely a bit less worn. Besides that she had the black mourning dress that the ladies at the hospice had made her a present of before her departure. For going down to Belluno she might wear that; but what underclothes could she take with her if she had nothing but two shirts all patched and darned to be ashamed of? There was nothing to count on among her mother's belongings. The only good piece there was the shawl; the remainder was made up of rags still more threadbare than her own.

She nonetheless opened the chest, and one by one she took in hand, spread out, and looked over these poor garments as well. They had the stiffness, color, and odor that the clothes of the dead have; and she took them in hand, studied them at length, put them down, picked them up once more. . . . In reality she herself was not aware of her own movements. She was not at all thinking of what she was doing. For several hours now she had been completely beside herself. She knew only that if suddenly she were told that her sister was dead, she would have experienced less anguish. Her whole being was rebelling in anguish. 'Not Rosùte! Not Rosùte! . . . '

All at once, in a corner of the chest her hands came upon the bottle of grappa that she had discovered in the straw mattress of the bed on the very day of their return to the hut after their stay at the hospice. She had hidden it, wrapped in a rag, among her belongings. She took it and looked at it; it was still almost half full of grappa. Only a few months had passed since the day on which she had found and hidden that bottle! . . . A few months, and yet how infinite a time and space separated then and now! . . . Although at that time she had just lost her mother, how much, how much less unhappy she had been then than today! She was still able to hope, then, to believe, to have faith. . . . She was not sick then. She had had Rosùte then!

The thought of her sister stabbed her heart, transfixing her anew. The next day at that hour the little one would be alone in the hut with Barbe Zef. . . . At the outset she would cry and be very unhappy without her. Then the weeks and the months would go by, and she would get used to it. . . . Until one day would come—she was certain of it!—the way it had come for her mamma, the way it had come for her. . . . One day. . . .

But . . . Rosùte, whose daughter was she? . . . Whose? When she was born, the true husband of their mother, Gaspari Zef, was no longer with them. . . . But the woman of Malga Varmost had spoken only of maternity aborted and suppressed. . . . Why had she not asked her? Why had she not probed deeper and dared to face the truth straight through to the bottom? . . . But of course Rosùte resembled *him*. She had *his* freckled skin, *his* red hair. . . . How come she had never noticed it before? How come she had never realized it? Yes, yes, Rosùte was the living image of Barbe Zef! . . .

The suspicion was not appearing for the first time to her in these days, but like an asp it bit her anew and horribly. . . . If it were indeed so! . . . She felt so deeply disturbed that she could hardly stand on her feet; and with her hands she pressed down on her heart, for it seemed to her that its beating could be heard beyond the walls. Some time passed like that. Meanwhile Barbe Zef was greasing his shoes and preparing the snowshoes for the next day's crossing.

When she went back into the kitchen, she was extremely pale but tranquil and, holding the bottle between her hands, she went directly to him and put it right in front of him.

'What is it?' he asked. 'Grappa? Where was it? And when did you find it?'

'In the straw mattress of the bed. Just this moment,' lied Mariutine.

The man took the bottle, recognized it, uncorked it, sniffed at it. Temptation was strong, but fear made him suspicious.

'And you, won't you drink a bit?' he asked, staring fixedly at Mariutine.

'If you give it to me,' she replied.

He held out the bottle to her so that she could put it to her mouth, but half way he changed his mind.

'Take a bowl,' he said.

Mariutine obeyed, and he himself poured her the grappa. She drank it in one gulp to the last drop and returned the empty bowl to him. Completely reassured, he pushed the bowl away again with his hand, put his mouth to the bottle, and gulped down a good swallow.

'Enough,' he said, putting the bottle back on the table. 'One doesn't drink, on the eve of the day when one has to hike. And you, go to sleep.'

She left him alone. Leaving the door ajar, she took off her shoes and stood barefoot in the dark with her back against the wall. And there she stayed. From time to time without a sound she came near the crack of the door to spy beyond. With anguish she saw the man always in the same place, in front of the bottle that little by little he was emptying, despite his good resolutions. But he continued to be awake and in full possession of himself, his eyes open. Hours passed. Dawn was perhaps not far off, and the time was coming to leave the hut, the time to depart.

Finally he began to babble to himself, to mutter, to tell

himself long inconclusive stories. She followed with her ear the scraping move that indicated the shifted position of the bench, the uncertain footsteps, the creaking of the straw mattress on which he was stretching out. And shortly afterwards a deep snore.

With wide-open eyes, livid, she let more time pass and then some more. From the kitchen always the same regular breathing. . . . Hours, minutes, seconds? . . .

A strange calm had descended on her. Above all it was necessary that Petòti should not bark. . . . But Petòti would never bark for her. . . .

Then ever so slowly, avoiding even the displacement of air around herself, with wary and deliberate movements, more creeping than walking, she widened the crack in the doorway and slipped into the kitchen.

He had extinguished the lantern, but a few brands still aglow in the fireplace sent forth flashes of light. In half darkness there he was. . . . His body on the straw mattress filled with dry leaves was distinctly visible. He lay there stretched full length. . . . The odor of that body struck her. She had never before noticed it, the odor of soaked rags, of decayed wood, of tobacco, and of wolf. He was there. . . . Defenseless, prostrate, in her power, and she was looking at him, spying upon him. . . .

How they shrieked, that night, the owls of Bosco Tagliato! . . .

An abrupt pity for him, for herself, for life and its common destiny made her feel weak kneed, and she drew back trembling toward the doorway from which she had entered. Pity for that being who was there on the ground and who from birth to death had also remained a beggar, a poor unhappy wretch born perhaps without guile, but whom poverty, promiscuity, solitude, absolute privation of all that can sweeten and elevate life, had brutalized and overwhelmed. Except for getting drunk and coupling with some female, what else had this wretch had in his life? . . . Nothing else, nothing else in the world, except hard work and suffering. . . . And now . . .

But she stiffened against her weakness. Rosùte! . . .

'Not Rosùte, not Rosùte, not Rosùte!'

The kitchen was so small that it was enough for her, without moving, to reach out her arm, her hand, and grasp hold of the axe that had been thrown onto a heap of wood at the corner of the fireplace.

She grasped it and raised it as high as she could.

The blade flashed in the shadow.

She took aim at his neck, and delivered the blow.

✳

Not a cry—only a gush of blood.

Volumes in
the European
Women
Writers Series
include:

Artemisia
By Anna Banti
Translated by
Shirley D'Ardia
Caracciolo

*Woman to
Woman*
By Marguerite
Duras
and Xavière
Gauthier
Translated
by Katherine
A. Jensen

Mother Death
By Jeanne
Hyvrard
Translated by
Laurie Edson

*On Our Own
Behalf:
Women's Tales
from Catalonia*
Edited
by Kathleen
McNerney

*Music from
a Blue Well*
By Torborg
Nedreaas
Translated
by Bibbi Lee

*Nothing Grows
by Moonlight*
By Torborg
Nedreaas
Translated
by Bibbi Lee

*Why Is There
Salt in the Sea?*
By Brigitte
Schwaiger
Translated by
Sieglinde Lug